Stepping into th

MOLLY WEIR

Stepping into the Spotlight

ARROW BOOKS

Arrow Books Ltd
3 Fitzroy Square, London W1

An imprint of the Hutchinson Publishing Group

London Melbourne Sydney Auckland
Wellington Johannesburg and agencies
throughout the world

First published Hutchinson & Co (Publishers) Ltd 1975
Arrow edition 1976
© Molly Weir 1975

Made and printed in Great Britain
by The Anchor Press Ltd
Tiptree, Essex

ISBN 0 09 914170 1

Dedicated to the memory of Miss Chree,
who enriched my life, and who made digs
in London home, until Sandy took over.

To live in hearts we leave behind is not to die.

Always do what you are afraid to do.
EMERSON

Luck is what happens when preparation meets opportunity.

I didn't realize it at the time, but getting into ITMA was the turning point of my acting life. If anyone had asked me, I would have told him with every confidence that my hopes were pinned on becoming an actress in the London theatre. Hadn't I toured with the great and beloved A. E. Matthews in *A Play for Ronnie* and hadn't I received a nod of approval from every single critic, in spite of the starry cast? True, we hadn't opened in London as we had hoped, but that was merely because the stars had refused to go on touring waiting for a free London theatre in the post-war boom when every play played to packed houses, and every peace-celebrating Londoner and soldier and visitor wanted to see anything and everything which was offered to them in the live theatre. Plays lucky enough to have opened when this mood of euphoria filled every heart, looked like running for ever. So, in my mind, radio work was a happy filler-in between theatre engagements.

I knew, of course, that ITMA wasn't just a radio show. It was an institution. It had blown away despair and heartache and defeat in great gusts of laughter during the harshest days of the war, and not only in Great Britain, but in every occupied country where brave people could hide a secret radio and risked death to listen to Tommy Handley cocking a snook at Hitler every Thursday night.

Looking back, I can see now that it was really ITMA which turned my footsteps permanently towards London, and everything that happened afterwards was because I would be for ever linked in the public mind with the greatest radio show of all time. I was lucky, because these were the great days of radio, when catch-phrases and the characters who uttered them became household names overnight, and the powerful habit of enslavement to the wireless, fostered during years of war, was still the strongest addiction in Britain and the free world.

And yet I was quite stunned by the excitement and near hysteria which followed when the news broke that the coming season would see ITMA with a new look. That three new members would be added to the cast to create new characters, but that three or four of the old ITMA stalwarts would be dropped. There were howls of anguish from loyal fans. 'What?' they shouted in their thousands, 'No more Mrs Mopp? No more "Can I do you now, sir?"', It's unthinkable. No more Naïve, with her adorable "What *is* kissing, Papa?" No more Ruby Rockcake with her raucous "No cups outside".' The newspapers had a bonanza, and printed letters by the score, bemoaning the disappearance of 'Funf', the wartime spy, of the polite salesman with his 'Good morning, nice day', of the seller of dirty postcards 'Very jolly. Oh golly', and all the many favourites bound up in the nostalgia of wartime memories.

When they'd exhausted all the arguments against change, they then turned with great excitement towards the identity of the three upstarts who had dared to usurp the places of the old favourites. The newspapers were after the unknown trio like cocks after grossets. They had never heard of any of us. Tony Francis was a young man who could make every conceivable sort of mechanical noise with his throat and was to play Reg Raspberry. Deryck Guyler, a Liverpudlian like Tommy Handley, was to be Dan Dungeon, the 'gloomy Scouser', to whom 'nobody never tells no one nothing', and I was to be Tattie McIntosh. We were to play all sorts of other little voices and characters, but these were the main names to start with.

Although I was fairly well known in Scotland by this time, thanks to the radio series *The McFlannels* and *Down at the Mains*, plus *Scottish Ballroom* and appearances with Ronnie Munro's variety orchestra, I was almost entirely unknown in London.

I was quite unprepared for the enthusiastic interest of the press in the smallest pieces of information about me. My landlady in Clapham was nearly driven out of her mind by impatient newsmen eager for an interview, who all had to be told that I was still in Scotland and was not expected to come south until just before the start of the new ITMA season. They could hardly believe their ears. What was Molly Weir doing away up there in the wilds of Scotland when they wanted to know every last thing about her? Poor Mrs Parker, pounding up three flights of stairs each time the telephone rang in my room, told one and all that I would be down on such-and-such a date, and not one minute before then. They couldn't believe anyone would hide from such heaven-sent publicity, and were quite sure they were dealing with an eccentric or a crafty pseudo-Garbo who was playing hard to get.

I was blissfully unaware of any of this, for in Scotland there wasn't very much enthusiasm. Some newspapers howked out pictures of me taken during the Carroll Levis shows, or at the Festival when I was in the pageant, or from the shorthand demonstration posters, and they asked a few polite questions, but they didn't exactly go mad or imply that I was about to set the Thames on fire. If my own folk could take it all so calmly, how could I possibly anticipate the frenzied interest which would greet me when at last I went down to London?

My husband and I decided that for this ITMA engagement I would spend nine days out of each fortnight in London. This would enable me to do two broadcasts and to come home for five days before returning for another nine days and another two broadcasts; because, of course, I couldn't afford to travel up and down every week and keep my room on in London, modest though the rent was. I was perhaps in radio's top show, but I was very small fry, and I wasn't earning the sort of money which would allow me to commute like an early David Frost. As it was, our friends and relatives thought I must be out of my mind even to contemplate that journey between London and Glasgow every nine days, and I must say there were times during that winter when I agreed with them, when I sat for endless hours in freezing overnight trains, waiting for frozen points to be thawed out, and not even a cup of hot tea to stop teeth from chattering. On one occasion, we didn't pull into Euston till two o'clock in the afternoon when we ought to have been there by 6.45 in the morning, and when I reached Clapham my landlady had been round to the chapel and had said three masses for the peace of my soul by that time! What my Presbyterian grannie and mother would have said to that, I dared not think. 'Oor Molly definitely fallen among the Philistines.'

But all that lay ahead. I was so thankful that Sandy was staying in our house in Thornliebank, for at least I needn't worry about emptying that cold-water tank, or worry about whether or not I'd locked all the doors and shut all the windows, and made sure there wasn't the tiniest spark left in the fireplace. And what a relief to the mind to know I needn't hump my entire wardrobe to London with me, but could have 'audience clothes' in Clapham, and change those around each time I came home after each pair of broadcasts. Not that my wardrobe was all that vast after years of wartime shortages, but it was comforting to know I could keep clothes in two cities. I thought this was the height of sophistication until I met a girl during a broadcast, and she had a flat in Paris as well as one in London! Now that really was something straight out of Somerset Maugham or Noël Coward, and made my Clapham flat seem very small beer. But it was mine, and by this time beautifully familiar, and I was greatly soothed by the knowledge that it was there for me to return to when the moment arrived for ITMA to launch itself into the next series with three new faces – one of them mine.

For the first show, I travelled down during the daytime, so that I would have a nice quiet evening arranging my wardrobe, and have the forenoon the following day for collecting my rations and organizing renewal of my registration with the dairy and the grocer, for we were still on ration books, and points and coupons, and were to remain so for several years. I had thought the end of the war would mean the end of ration books, but it was to take a long time before we could regard those tattered prized booklets as relics.

Mrs Parker panted upstairs as soon as she knew I had arrived, and regaled me with news of the siege she'd endured, hardly daring to go outside the house for fear of being accosted yet again by veritable posses of newsmen. I was absolutely flabbergasted. 'They're coming tomorrow morning,' she informed me, 'to take photographs of you in the flat.' I stared at her disbelievingly.

'But why?' I said. It was her turn to shake her head in some perplexity.

'Because,' she said, slowly and clearly, as if speaking to some dim-wit, 'everybody is dying to see what you look like. They have pictures of the other two, because they're both in London, but nobody has seen you, and to be in ITMA is nearly to be as important as to be a member of the Royal Family.'

I burst out laughing. 'Well,' I said, 'I've got to get my rations in tomorrow, and I have a rehearsal at four o' clock, and I've just got no time for photographers, and the ITMA folk might not like it anyway.' That was what I thought. Next morning, before I'd even brushed my hair, poor Mrs Parker was holding them at bay on the doorstep. I heard the commotion before she called upstairs to me to tell me she'd put them in the drawing room, for they wouldn't budge until they'd seen me, spoken to me, and taken pictures. I took time to have some tea and toast, put on my nice navy-blue linen suit made by my dear wee dressmaker in Glasgow, Mrs Campbell, and went downstairs. They were enchanted to discover that I spoke real Scots, was so wee, and so bewildered by their interest. If I'd appeared in kilt, sporran and buckled shoes, with heather sticking out of my ears, they couldn't have been more delighted. They took pictures of me sitting at Mrs Parker's grand piano – me, who never got beyond sixpenny piano lessons! They took pictures of Mrs P. and me sitting sipping tea out of her best china, of which I'd not caught so much as a glimpse until that moment. I was photographed in her tiny kitchen, filling the kettle, and stirring something in a pot. At the typewriter in my room. Picking up the phone, pretending I was listening to Ted Kavanagh with script instructions. In the street with shopping basket, *en route* to the shops (at least it enabled me to collect my rations). Registering at the dairy. At the grocer's. Fondling somebody else's dog in the street. And putting my kĕy in the front door, laden with my shopping. When they couldn't think of another single pose, they vanished, telling me they'd see me later at rehearsal for pictures with the entire cast.

On the way to that first 4 p.m. rehearsal, when I would meet the rest of the cast for the first time, I bought the early edition of the *Standard* and there large as life was I, shopping basket at my feet, putting my key in the front door of the digs in Clapham, and the words underneath said, 'You'll hear from wee Molly on Thursday', and beside it another one of me patting the strange dog, 'Molly Weir stops to greet a friend'. And that was the first trickle of the flood of publicity which followed me during the whole of the time I was privileged to work in the star-studded fun factory which was ITMA.

The commissionaire at the door of the Paris Cinema, where we rehearsed and broadcast from, stared hard at me when I told him who I was. Everybody tried to gate-crash the ITMA rehearsals, and he was none too sure he ought to let me in until Ted Kavanagh appeared and vouched for me. I felt very shy and nervous and more than a little apprehensive as I went down the stairs I was to come to know as well as my own front door in later years, and I was handed over to Tina, Francis Worsley's secretary, who whisked me off to the ladies' room and showed me where to hang my coat and hat and tidy my hair in preparation for the photo session. It was like the first day at a new school.

Then it was into the studio, where Tommy and Francis already stood chatting with photographers, and the others drifted in one by one. Diana Morrison, the redoubtable 'Hotchkiss' who ruled Tommy's life with a rod of iron in the series, turned out to be a tall handsome lady with dark short hair, very country-life-style with beautiful tweeds and an elegant manner. Lind Joyce, the singer, with thick black fringe and long page-boy bob, looked Oriental and actressy, and I felt very ordinary and humdrum beside her, and not a bit like a professional performer at all. I could see I'd have to do something about my clothes, as this was an 'audience' show, and my wartime leftovers weren't a patch on the outfits I was now looking at with covetous eyes! Jack Train, the beloved Colonel Chinstrap, greeted me with a wide grin, and immediately plunged into a series of jokes with Tommy, Francis and the photographers. I was to discover Jack had a fund of new stories every week, and no rehearsal could start until he had us rolling with laughter over his latest outrageous joke. Hugh Morton, elegant and friendly, was introduced (I'd always loved his 'Would you care for a sninch of puff' sort of Malapropisms), then Fred Yule, the gorgeous bass-baritone who was Bigga-Banga, the Tomptopian Chieftain, came over and warmly welcomed me to the team. Only then did I realize that the two men hovering near me were the other newcomers: Deryck Guyler, later to become one of the best-known and best-loved character actors both on radio and TV, although, like me, he thought he was just having a temporary stab at light-entertainment radio between stage engagements; and Tony Francis, the lad with the versatile throat which could produce mechanical sounds which defied comparison with the real thing.

The photographers arranged us in groups; the old cast, the new trio by themselves, all together, the ladies separately, then the gentlemen separately. Then with producer and writer. Then producer, writer and Tommy together. Then with the orchestra. It went on for nearly an hour, and only when Francis looked at his watch and said 'That'll have to do for today, gentlemen' did they vanish and leave us to get on with the rehearsal. It was an ordeal to speak my first line in my Scottish voice before such an experienced and famous cast, and I never lifted my eyes from my script until my part was over. I knew now why Ted Kavanagh had asked me at the time of our first meeting if I knew what a Tattie Bogle was, and I'd answered that it was a scarecrow, for my name in the show was Tattie McIntosh. My very first line in that famous show was 'He sits there in Castle-Wee-House and he'll no' come oot, and he expects me to pour his porridge under his wee door. Och he's daft!' That was to be my catchphrase, in various forms, 'Och your're daft', or 'Och he's daft', followed by a light ripple of laughter. I always like to give a very individual laugh for any variety character I devise, and for Tattie I rippled up the scale like a tinkling bell (I hoped!). Anyway, they liked it, and it stayed in.

Deryck Guyler seemed very quiet and vague, and as apprehensive as I felt, for his eyes met mine and he cast them upwards in half-fun, half-earnest terror, and put his hand over his diaphragm. I knew how he felt! Tony Francis was pink with excitement as he went through his snorts and whistles and saw-sounds, and although he was brilliant, I wondered in my heart how they were going to fit him into the show, and how to convince the listeners that it was indeed all done without artificial aids. I was later proved right in my fears for poor Tony, because they discovered when listening to the show that the sounds were so true to the real mechanical noises that nobody could tell that a human throat had made them, so out went Tony at the end of his six weeks' trial contract. I felt so sorry for him, for it was not his fault that he had failed – he was just too good.

Actually I hadn't realized we newcomers were only booked on a six weeks' trial basis, to be renewed or cancelled as events dictated. Having been booked through Ted Kavanagh, I hadn't troubled to read the small print too accurately, and assumed I was with them for the whole series. Tony's departure made my heart jump, and also made me thankful that I seemed to have gone down pretty well with audience and wider public alike. The first night of the new series was electrifying. We'd done two hours the day before, following the photographic session, then next day, on the Thursday, we met at three o'clock and worked with the orchestra at the mikes, rehearsing, cutting, pruning until it was timed to the last second. For, of course, we went out 'live' at 8.30 p.m. on Thursdays, and had to finish within our allotted half-hour, before the chimes of Big Ben for nine o'clock.

We broke rehearsal at six or thereabouts, and went our ways, either out to a restaurant for dinner, or back to the communal dressing room for a sandwich, and returned at eight o'clock to the studio for final check-up of our appearance, and any last-minute alterations to the script, depending on whether or not anything significant had been in the latest editions of the newspapers. I felt far too terrified to think of eating, but Hugh Morton insisted I accompany him to a little restaurant off Jermyn Street (very posh!) and have a light meal to sustain me through the evening. This was to set the pattern of our ways during the whole series, and for the first time in my life I was dining in style before a performance. I hardly uttered a word during that first meal, although Hugh tried to put me at my ease, for he was a well-seasoned ITMA trouper and assured me the public were on our side and longing for our return to the air. It was all very well for him. They knew him and approved of him. What would they think of me, when they were probably dying to hear Mrs Mopp or Naïve? And how would my Scottish voice fit into such an English show? This wasn't merely another radio performance – it was a trial – and the jury were the entire British nation! And there was no opportunity for correcting mistakes, for each word went on the air as it was spoken.

Back at the Paris, the air buzzed with excitement. Tickets were carefully checked, and old friends greeted one another and congratulated each other on their luck in being present for the first of the new series, with the new-look cast. Tommy paced nervously back and forth at the back of the orchestra, as Rae Jenkins took his place in front of it.

Ted Kavanagh, plump, red-haired and apparently calm, took the centre of the stage and did a magnificent 'warm-up' of the audience, and then we trooped on, and sat down on two rows of chairs facing one another, ladies on the left, gentlemen on the right. We were introduced to the audience one by one, rose and took a bow to applause, then a tense hush fell as the red light winked, a hand was held warningly by Rae to alert the orchestra, and on a 'green' light we were at the mike and singing the words which had cheered Britain and Europe for how many years? 'It's that man again, it's that man again, yes that Tommy Handley is here.' I could hardly get the words out for the emotional lump which filled my throat. Fancy me actually standing on this stage singing those immortal words! In ITMA! Could I be dreaming, after all? No I wasn't – the applause would have wakened me up, for it came like thunder after that opening chorus, and then there was no time to think of anything but cues and words and waiting for laughs. For quite the worst thing anyone can do in such a show is 'tread' on laughs, and thus silence the audience into stopping laughing for fear of missing anything spoken over their reactions. Timing is all-important. Sensing that split-second's waiting to see if they're going to see the joke, and riding smoothly on if the laugh doesn't come, so the show keeps buoyant. One mustn't lose concentration for a second, and at the end I felt as limp as a rag – or a wet dish-cloot, as my mother would have said. The applause rose, and it was right on the tick of nine o'clock. It was over. My début with the best that radio could offer. I hadn't fallen on my face, and I hadn't killed any laughs. More than that I couldn't say. Ted Kavanagh sent a glow through my heart by coming over to me at once and telling me my timing had been excellent, and my characterization delightful. So that was all right. No writer says such words if you've ruined his comedy! Not even to be polite! But Hugh Morton's delightful wife Monica gave me a very good piece of advice, which I followed, for I saw that she was right. The audience milled round us for autographs and seemed pleased with the new brooms, but Monica took me aside and gazed at me earnestly and asked if she might just suggest something which she thought would improve my performance. My heart jumped. What had I done wrong? Were the others just being kind, even Ted, when they'd approved of Tattie? 'Yes,' I said, trembling, 'What is it?' 'Well,' she said softly, 'I think you could afford to attack more. The voice and the character are appealing, but against the "ponging" style of the regulars you are much too gentle, and tend to be swamped.' How about that, eh? 'Gentle', my mother's favourite word, applied to my style. I felt a sort of ladylike languor steal over me at the mere thought of having conveyed such an effect. Then I shook myself. Monica was dead right – I knew in my bones she was, and I confirmed it when I listened to the repeat, and from then on stifled the shy awareness that I was a strange voice in a familiar show, and 'ponged' it out with the best of them. And enjoyed myself into the bargain, *and* was accepted into full fellowship with the team.

Tommy found great amusement in my not minding being called 'Tattie', a somewhat derogatory description in England, and that was his name for me from first to last. Never Molly, always Tattie. I, of course, coming from the land of sporrans, haggis, kilts and bagpipes, was a natural target for his lively humour. He was always kind, but he knew I could take it, and I even actively encouraged him just to hear the hotch-potch of Scots–English falling from his lips.

I remember once we were giving a show for a group of naval officers stationed in Lady Peel's house in the country, and Tommy noticed with amusement that a tall fair officer seemed particularly interested in my company. Actually, if he'd but known it, we were discussing the difficulty of getting fresh eggs and the be-ribboned gallant was telling me he might be able to get some from the farm at home! Anyway, when we got into the bus for our homeward journey, Tommy turned to me roguishly and said, 'Aye, aye, Tattie, you fairly bewitched that young officer – I saw you, you wee Scotch MacSporran.'

'Tommy,' I turned in shocked surprise, 'do you know who that was? That was Gordon of Fochabers.'

'Gordon of Fochabers,' he laughed, '*Gordon of Fochabers!*'; and as he rolled his tongue round the new lovely syllables, I could see he had added this phrase to his collection. For weeks afterwards, when I came into rehearsal, he would shout joyously, 'Hu-llo, Tattie, and how is Gordon of Fochabers these days?', and any reply I might have made was drowned in the laughter of the rest of the cast and of Tommy himself.

He was a voracious reader, with an extensive vocabulary, and the idioms peculiar to the various parts of Britain were a delight to him. That was why he loved to introduce in the programme such Liverpool words as 'Scouse' and 'Whacker', and I noticed his eyes always shone with amusement in the scenes with Frisby Dyke, played by Deryck Guyler, his fellow Liverpudlian. In those days the use of such words was very daring, and I think it gave him a pleasant sense of outrage to use such robust language within the sacred precincts of 'the spoken word'.

It was a never-failing source of wonder to Tommy that people daily mispronounced quite ordinary words without pausing to consider that they might be wrong. I first discovered this when he came into rehearsal one day, pipe between his teeth as usual, and said, 'Isn't it odd the number of people who say "partitularly"? I wonder if they ever *see* the letters when they read the word in print, or if they're so convinced it is "partitularly" that they imagine a "t" where there is a "c"?' He gazed into space, bemused, and, of course, when one of us asked why he mentioned it this afternoon he replied with a twinkle, 'Oh nothing in partitular.'

Another regular mispronouncement which fascinated him was 'Hippydrone' for 'Hippodrome'. He himself was so fastidious about words and pronunciation that it just didn't seem possible that people could see it written in huge letters over the theatre, and possibly all over their programmes, and yet persist in seeing a 'y' for an 'o' and an 'n' for an 'm'. He always referred to the 'Hippydrone', eyes alight with fun, just to see if anyone would pull him up.

Anyone who listened to the programmes must have been struck by the amount of comedy which was extracted simply from words. There was the quick-talking woman who gabbled nonsense so furiously that Tommy had only time for one-word exclamations and ejaculations. There was the man who 'wisted his twords', and there was the irrepressible Frisby Dyke, of course, who kept asking, in mystified tones, 'What's a catastrophe?' or 'What's a cacophony?' And, above all, there was always Tommy's glorious use and misuse of words, ordinary ones, invented ones, and hopelessly entangled ones.

His inventiveness was unique. He used to spin me long impossible stories about a troupe of musical acrobats whom he christened 'The McGibblybites', who travelled on an india-rubber bus with elastic sides which expanded to take their instruments. The tales of this family's adventures enlivened many a weary journey when we did shows for various charities.

Once, in the midst of this continuing saga of the McGibblybites, he broke off so spontaneously that I had no suspicion that it might be another leg-pull, for I was very naïve and had a reputation for believing anything that was said to me.

'Whatever became of that chap Frou-Frou who was such a sensation at the Prince of Wales Theatre a few years ago?' he called out to Francis Worsley, our producer.

'Frou-Frou?' said Francis, playing for time, as I realized much much later.

'Who was Frou-Frou?' I asked eagerly, always anxious to learn everything about this glamorous world I'd now entered.

Tommy no doubt had winked to the others, for now they all took it up. It was, after all, a very dull journey into dreary rain-sodden countryside where we were to do our charity show. They must have been glad of any diversion. 'Do you mean to say you've never heard of Frou-Frou? Well – we knew Scotland was a backward country, but I thought his name would be known even up there.'

I was indignant, but I hadn't heard of him so could say nothing. I felt terribly ignorant.

'He was a household word,' from somebody else. 'You *must* have heard of him.'

'But what did he *do*?' I asked in exasperation.

'Well,' said Tommy, 'there was this enormous tin whistle on the stage, running right up into the flies, and Frou-Frou climbed up inside it, and showed his bottom at each aperture, where the fingers would have produced the notes.'

I sat in stunned silence.

'And was that all?' I asked eventually, wondering if I had missed anything.

'It was enough,' said Tommy, 'it was most original. He had a very expressive bottom, and he was the toast of London.'

I believed every word.

Until about three years ago when we were discussing Tommy's wilder inventions, and Hugh Morton (Brigadier Dear) said to me, 'I'll never forget how funny you were about Frou-Frou and that tin-whistle act Tommy invented.'

I stopped dead in my tracks in Jermyn Street. 'Wasn't it true?' I asked in blank amazement. Hugh laughed so loud he nearly stopped the traffic.

'Don't say you've believed that all those years?'

'Every single word,' I said. I must admit I had thought it was a daft sort of performance, but then I had often noticed that Londoners laughed at things we'd think mad north of the border.

And what Tommy invented as a joke to pass a tedious journey almost came true, after all, when the much-publicized Japanese Yoko came to London and held auditions for bottoms. She intended making a film simply of that part of the anatomy, because she thought she could find such variety and expressiveness in individual bottoms! And she was taken quite seriously. No wonder 'that man' made a nation laugh through years of wartime miseries. He was *years* ahead of his time.

But I didn't have to invent anything to make *him* laugh. Once, when we were discussing how the various parts of our body were developed because of the use we made of them, like the diaphragms of singers and the feet of ballet dancers, I said, using the broad Scots words because I knew they would amuse him, 'Aye, I've done a lot of cycling and dancing and walking, and that's why I've got such sturdy hurdies.' In the explosion of laughter which followed, I translated that this simply meant solid thighs. I'd already taught Tommy that a spurtle was a stick we used for stirring the porridge. And without a pause he sent the cast into uproar by calling out in broadest 'Scouse', 'Awa' wi' ye, Tattie, or I'll tak' a spurtle to your sturdy hurdies.' I was a bit sorry I'd said this, all the same, for whenever I attempted to be serious in the future, Tommy would look at me with exaggerated concern and say, 'And how are your sturdy hurdies today then, Tattie?' and my argument was lost.

He really had a lightning sense of fun. I'll never forget his opening the newspaper one day and saying, 'Oh I see wee Georgie Wood's had to leave the pantomime because he's down with appendicitis.'

'Where is he?' somebody asked. 'We must send him a card.'

'Where do you think?' replied Tommy, without a second's pause. 'The dolls' hospital, of course!'

I never read Georgie Wood's column in *The Stage* without thinking of Tommy's quip, and hearing again the laughter which followed.

2

The newspapers may have said of us, 'Three newcomers are rapidly carving a niche for themselves in ITMA,' and the public down south may have put a feather in our hats by making us feel we had successfully replaced their old favourites, but when I went back to Glasgow after the first two ITMA broadcasts I was brought down to earth with a thud. 'They didnae gi'e ye much to do,' was the general comment. They'd been used to my playing leading parts in the Scottish shows, and were unimpressed that a couple of words in ITMA which went round the world were of more significance to a radio career than an entire play heard only in our own much-loved but small country. For the first time I understood the dilemma of the choice as to whether it was better to be a large frog in a small puddle or a small frog in a large pond. My friends and family were in no doubt that I'd made the wrong choice.

But it was great to be home again, and Sandy was deaved with my excited descriptions of the enthusiasm shown by the London press and public for our show, and of the huge queues which stretched right round the Paris Cinema for over an hour before the doors opened. Tickets were issued, and were greatly coveted, but apart from a few reserved seats for VIPs, it was first-come-first-served as to where one sat, and there was great eagerness to be as near the front as possible, to savour every glance, every wink, almost within touching distance of the cast. And at the end they surged in droves towards the stage for our autographs.

'Did anybody ask for yours?' my mother queried, when I told her all this.

'Of course!' I replied indignantly. 'I'm one of the cast.'

'Well, for a' they gi'e ye to say,' she said quenchingly, 'it's hardly worth while gaun doon a' that road.' Visiting London was like preparing for a trip to Australia, in my mother's eyes, and she was aghast that I could contemplate such a journey every nine days. 'But you're that heidstrong,' she said, 'and Sandy just gi'es ye a' yer ain way.'

That wasn't quite true, for Sandy welcomed me home as a housewife even more than as an actress who was making for herself a wee corner in the world of show business. He declared, 'If I didn't miss you for yourself, I'd miss you for your cooking.' He was delighted to down tools and have his menus selected by me, and not to have to think of food or rations for five whole days until he saw it all ready on his plate. It was like leading a double life, a sort of Jekyll-and-Hyde situation, where I was transformed on the overnight journey from London to a douce Glasgow wife and house-keeper. Washings were done, floors were cleaned, fresh curtains hung, visitors entertained, and huge bakings done to fill the tins against the day of my departure for the south again. The train attendants began to recognize me, the Scots ones intrigued to find Ivy McTweed of the Mc-Flannels in the sleeper, the English enchanted to discover Tattie of ITMA in their midst.

It was just as well that Glasgow kept my feet on the ground, for it would have been only too easy to get an exaggerated idea of my own importance. Invitations flooded in from all sides to entertain the ITMA cast, and although I had been miles away in my war factory when

Tommy and his company had kept up the spirits of the free world during the war, I was included in the generous euphoria in which we bathed. A millionaire owner of the Tote Racing Syndicate gave a dinner for us at the Savoy after the show one night, and the two most impressive things which fairly stunned me were that we had nine waiters for fourteen of us, and that in the next room my beloved Winston Churchill was dining with the wartime Cabinet members! Oh, I longed to peep round the doors to see my hero in the flesh, and was only restrained by the instinct that this would not have been at all seemly behaviour from someone who was wining and dining in one of the famous River rooms.

It was at that dinner that I tasted my first Martini and didn't like it one little bit. As a Rechabite I had a great fear of strong drink, and I'd seen enough drunkenness in Springburn to make me exceedingly wary of all liquor under whatever fancy name it was disguised. Anyway, it tasted 'wersh' to my palate, which, like most teetotallers, preferred something sweeter. Champagne flowed throughout the meal, but it was the food which made me realize I was indeed dining as the guest of a millionaire. After years of rationing, the lavishness of that meal was like something out of the Arabian Nights. We started off with *hors d'oeuvres* of such complexity and variety that it would have sufficed me, with nothing else added. Then followed a *whole* spring chicken each! It broke my heart to have to leave half of it, for my ration-trained stomach simply wasn't used to coping with such amounts. I'd have made that wee bird last for a week if I'd been able to buy one outside this palatial establishment. There was fresh salad to go with it, and crisp roast potatoes, not to mention fresh rolls and butter. Next came strawberries – in wintertime – with meringues and cream. And there were delicious *petits fours* with the coffee. Huge glasses were filled with a golden liquid, and I was so thirsty by this time that I drank it as greedily as I had the iced drink of Mr Crawford's the night he'd taken me to the gallery to see *The Mikado*.[1] But this was no iced drink. I didn't know it, but I was downing Napoleon brandy by the glassful! Francis Worsley, across the table, seemed to have a very strange expression on his face, and although I was normally very shy of him and not a little afraid, I found myself giggling and waving to him to let him know how much I was enjoying myself.

He told me next day that he had been aghast to see me drinking this nectar like ginger pop and he knew I hadn't the least idea what it was, but he was unable to say a word because our host had moved round to sit beside me at this stage of the meal and was so entranced by my Scottish accent that Francis couldn't break up our tête-à-tête to steer me away to a safe corner of the room.

But at the end of the party, when we went through the ballroom where Carroll Gibbons still played softly to some late revellers, and the air hit me, my legs folded under me. What was the matter? I couldn't understand it. My head swam, and I had no control over my limbs. Francis, worried sick over the effects of all this unaccustomed drink on my little Rechabite stomach, walked me up and down in the icy night air until a taxi came, and he bade Deryck Guyler see me home to the digs in Clapham, and not to leave until he'd seen me safely into my room. I giggled feebly at the mere idea of Mrs Parker allowing a gentleman upstairs at that hour of the morning, and subsided thankfully into the comfort of the upholstery of the taxi. Deryck shook me awake when we were reaching Clapham. 'Where is your street, Molly?' he said. I raised my head, and quickly lowered it again. I felt terrible. 'Molly, where is your street?'

1. *Best Foot Forward*

Cautiously I lifted my head slowly, and thought I vaguely recognized the corner near the Plough.

'Round that corner,' I said through closed teeth. I wouldn't acknowledge the awareness which teetered at the edge of my mind. I couldn't be drunk. I simply couldn't. I hadn't touched the champagne and I'd only had one wee sip of that sour Martini. That stuff at the end of the meal had been too nice to be dangerous.

The taxi stopped and Deryck took my key and opened the door quietly. But I was sober enough to refuse to allow him to assist me up the stairs and have Mrs Parker rise from her puritan couch like an avenging angel. He was so nice, Deryck. And so kind. I was lucky to have been in charge of such a fine person, and I knew he was a very good man because he used to sit at the back of the Paris and study his bible during rehearsals. He must have been terribly shocked by my behaviour, as I was myself now, although I couldn't understand how it had happened.

Sheer will-power got me up to the top flat. I almost flew up, lightly touching wall and railing with finger-tips to balance me, and moving as silently as a ghost. I reached my room, and only the thought of nice Lois next door gave me the strength to take off my clothes. I *longed* for bed and a respite from this rocking and seething which made me feel as though I were on a ship. But I couldn't have Lois come into my room in the morning and find me fully dressed in bed. So, shuddering against the rocking of the room, I dropped my clothes where I stood, taking great care not to move too quickly, turned out the light, and crept between the sheets. By the time I'd pulled the bedclothes round my shoulders, I was fast asleep.

In the morning I came to, as from a great great distance, and my hands were precisely where I'd laid them, curled round the sheets, and not a hair of the blankets was out of place. I'd lain like a felled ox without stirring all night. I lifted my head and the room spun round. 'Oh *no*,' I groaned, 'don't say it's going to start all over again.' The telephone rang and it was Francis Worsley. Thank goodness the instrument was by my bed or I could never have moved to answer it. He wanted to know how I was. I was to come straight to his office the moment I had breakfast, and he would give me Alka-Seltzers to remove the worst feeling of hangover. Me with a hangover! It was the first time in my life the word had been applied to me and the first time I'd heard of Alka-Seltzers.

Tommy and I were to appear at Earls Court that afternoon and Francis wanted to make sure I was fit to travel and fit to make a public appearance. I'd forgotten all about it. I struggled to a sitting position and tottered over to the mirror, curious and interested to see what signs of debauchery would show on my face. To my intense surprise, my face was calm and pale as a nun's, and I hadn't even been punished by having bloodshot eyes. How was it possible to be so wicked and show so little sign of it? I knew now I had been intoxicated for the first and only time in my life, and the experience was so ghastly I couldn't for the rest of my existence ever wish to repeat it. And I never have. How anyone could deliberately expose himself to this sort of misery is beyond my understanding. In my case, the lesson was well learned, and never forgotten. Never again would I drink anything without first enquiring what it was, and never again would I take more than one drink of *anything*, however mild. I may say that from that day forth I was known as 'One drink Tattie', for nobody could persuade me to accept more than one for all of my time in London.

I felt very thankful that nobody in the house suspected my fall from grace, and very ashamed to meet Francis Worsley's eye when I walked into his office later that morning. He drew a bottle from the desk drawer, dropped two fizzing tablets into a glass of water and when they'd dissolved bade me drink up. The worry was clearing from his face when he saw I was pale but still in one piece, and he could now laugh as he told me of my unappreciative swilling of the best Napoleon brandy. He shook his head smilingly. 'I'll never be able to look Carroll Gibbons in the face again,' he said, 'after sneaking out of the back door of the Savoy with a fu' Scot on my arm.'

I kept my lowered eyes on my drink and said nothing, for I was too mortified to speak. Tommy arrived just then, patted my shoulder and said he hoped I was up to facing the multitudes, for he and I were representing ITMA at Earls Court for the next two or three hours. The place was seething when we arrived, and it took a posse of body-guards to escort us to the autograph-signing dais, which was roped off to prevent us from being trampled underfoot by the fans. The moment the loudspeakers announced that we would sign autographs, it was like a stampede. Everybody in the place, it seemed, wanted to see 'That Man' in the flesh, and the new wee Scots lassie. Books were thrust under our noses, hands were pushed under and over the rope to shake ours, photographers blazed away with their flash cameras, but thanks to that blessed fizzy drink my stomach had settled, and apart from a slight sensation of dizziness, I felt fine, if overwhelmed. It was my first experience of mass enthusiasm, and I think I'd have been much more frightened if I hadn't been almost entirely absorbed in concentrating on my physical well-being after the orgy of the night before. Truly all things are mixed with mercy.

The body-guards escorted us round the Exhibition, and at every single stand a whisper behind a cupped hand from the exhibitor told me that I'd find a drink behind the curtain!

A drink! I shuddered at the mere idea. I dutifully went behind the first curtain, just to pretend I was interested, and the smell of the stuff in the glass sent my stomach rocking, and I came out again so fast the man must have thought I had knocked the beverage back like a veteran. I laughed afterwards at the mental picture of untouched glasses of liquor sitting behind the curtains of all the stands I had visited that day, and the puzzled faces of all those who had had their generous hospitality ignored.

At each stand we were given a memento of our visit, and it was like having free access to Santa's grotto. Nothing like this had ever happened to me. To be rewarded just for being *me*, or rather just for being *Tattie*, because the mere fact of my presence, with Tommy, ensured a public for the stands at which we appeared. By the end of the afternoon I had a man in attendance just to carry the gifts. An electric iron, complete with temperature regulator, among the first of its kind. A lovely ruby-red plastic fruit bowl, an artistic example of the possibilities of plastics. A potato peeler, a bedside clock, a fountain pen, and a mass of tiny samples of the newest foods. After years of austerity this was corn in Egypt and was almost too much to accept without guilty feelings of greed. I had been brought up to believe that moderation in all things was desirable, and my Presbyterian background made me unable to receive such lavish generosity without a sense of shame for being so acquisitive.

But the iron was a joy, nevertheless, and made a great job of Sandy's shirts when I carried it home in triumph on my next visit. I had always been terrified of scorching the collars, a danger instantly removed now I had this splendid iron with its inbuilt temperature regulator. And the red plastic bowl looked rich and cheerful against the light in the dining room, where it complemented all the other little touches of red I had there. I may say I have the bowl to this day, a souvenir of my first public appearance with the great Tommy Handley.

I had intended going home for Christmas and New Year, and to pot with expense, for we felt it would be more comfortable in our own house at the Festive Season than living in my one-room digs in Clapham, but as luck would have it I was invited to appear on television with Leslie Henson and Fred Emney in their Christmas revue. Television! For the first time! This was one of the reasons why I'd decided to come to London in the first place, because it offered opportunities for TV as well as films and theatre. I'd never met either Leslie Henson or Fred Emney, both big names in show business, and I was in my usual state of stomach-turning nerves at the prospect of working with them. I rang Sandy, who agreed I ought to do it, and he'd come down to London to be with me instead of my making the journey north. It wouldn't matter for one year, and I'd go home as near to the New Year as the following ITMA performance permitted.

It was decided I'd do the revue number from the Glasgow show 'Please, Captain, I've Swallowed my Whistle' and also take part in the Henson/Emney sketch 'The Green Eye of the Little Yellow God', and I was to be at Alexandra Palace at 10 a.m. It was back to the world of variety once more, with everybody knowing his own act, or rehearsing separately and meeting for the first time on 'the day'.

It was on this bill that I met Jean Kent for the first time, and I was as excited as my own tremors would allow me to be, to meet the film star in the flesh. She wore a magnificent amethyst and gold collar necklace with matching bracelets and ear-rings, and was so friendly and pleased when I admired them that not only did she tell me where she'd bought them, but how much she paid for them! I'd never expected such a chummy confiding attitude from somebody from the silver screen. Joy Nichols and her brother were also on the bill, and Joy was later to be a very big name indeed in *Take It from Here*. They had just arrived from Australia and were then taking the first exploratory steps in English show-biz and I thought they were terrific.

There was a conjuror from Aberdeen, hardened to the demands of variety and not the least bit bothered about TV, who had so little understanding of my fears that he kept chatting to me about Hogmanay, and his various theatre dates. I must have looked considerably calmer than I felt when he actually expected me to respond to his blethers. Worse than that, another man, a stranger, kept coming up to me and engaging me in conversation, while I was trying to concentrate on my words, and on the various little snippets I had to do in the other sketches, for I discovered I had been fitted into another one, apart from 'The Green Eye of the Little Yellow God'. 'Take that man away, Sandy,' I hissed to my husband, 'or every word will fly out of my head. This is live television, and I've just *got* to concentrate.'

So Sandy led him away, and he told me afterwards he was sure the man thought I was being toffee-nosed in not wanting to spend my time with him, for he naturally thought that if I was good enough to be in ITMA I must be devoid of nerves, and that a first telly could be taken in my stride! That was what *he* thought. He was only behind the scenes, seeing how we all ticked, for he was an embryonic TV director. He never forgave me for what he obviously considered my stand-offishness when I was a 'big' name and he a beginner, for when he became a top director he, to use my mother's words, 'never looked the road I was on' and never employed me once. Personally I don't know how anybody so insensitive to the nerves of an actor ever became a successful director. I was sorry, though, that he had misjudged me, and even more sorry that I hadn't the sophistication to tell him that I needed absolute quietness before such an ordeal.

And an ordeal it certainly was. It was early days for TV and the cameras were enormous things without the complicated lenses used nowadays when close-ups and mid-shots can be undertaken from half-way across the studio. In 1947 if the camera wanted a close shot it brought the huge plate-glass front to within inches of one's nose. When I went into 'Please, Captain' at the dress rehearsal, I found to my horror that this plate-glass reflected my face upside down and I was staring up into my bottom teeth! The sight so unnerved me that I almost forgot my words, and I dreaded having to repeat this experience on the real show.

I was pleased to note that the 'big' names, and they were really big, not a little tiddler like me, were equally nervous and silent as they paced about waiting for the show to start, and I remembered the words of my dear Miss Mitchell, my first elocution teacher, who, observing my silent pacing before her annual show for her pupils, told me that it was a sure sign of an artistic temperament and I might just have a future in the theatre.[2] Although, in another way, the silent tension of the stars dismayed me, for it confirmed what I was beginning to suspect, that this highly nervous condition before a show was never going to diminish and was the price I'd have to pay to be a performer. And I was right. I feel the same today as I did then, and have come to accept that the butterflies are in permanent residence in my stomach.

Everything about that first television show felt unreal, even the presence of Sandy back-stage, which was far from normal, for I usually dislike anyone close to me when I'm

2. *Best Foot Forward*

working. However, I must have done all right, for this show was followed by quite a number of television engagements from 'Ally Pally', as Alexandra Palace was affectionately called, and I happily mixed revue, variety appearances and plays, and grew very fond of that part of London and my work there. I did quite a lot of singing in those variety and revue engagements, and again was secure and happy in the knowledge that the musicians who played for me were the best.

On one occasion I was persuaded to promise to go on to a big charity ball at the Dorchester when I'd finished at Ally Pally and it turned out to be a real pea-souper, with fog so thick that traffic was almost at a standstill. Nowadays, I'd simply have realized that nobody would have expected me to turn up from the other side of London on such a night, nor missed me if I had been absent, but then, having promised, I felt they would all be waiting for me and would feel betrayed if I broke my word. It took *hours* to get to the Dorchester, and I shared a taxi with Peter Waring, who thought I must be out of my mind to bother to attend such a function on such a night. However, Michael Tippett, who had invited me, was hovering in the hall when I arrived and so glad to see me that I was rewarded for any effort I made to be there. I flew into the ladies' room and jumped into my blue velvet evening dress, ran a comb through my hair, and slipped into my place at one of the long tables next to Benjamin Britten. Their names meant little to me then, and to me they were just a very jolly crowd who had a warm and riotous welcome for me, and who toasted the Scots for being 'always dependable'. Apparently the fog had prevented a lot of other 'names' from turning up. So, after the dinner, there I was on a dais with Christopher Stone, the famous spinner of gramophone records who was a household name, with a voice which sent a ripple of delighted anticipation through one when it floated from the radio. I was fascinated to be his assistant in the drawing of raffles, the auctioning of expensive gifts, and all the other fund-raising ploys for which our help was enlisted. It was great fun, and I was well repaid when at the end they insisted on sending me home by car all the way to Clapham, so I didn't have to find my way by bus through the fog at the end of a long tiring day.

Every time I see those famous musicians I wonder if they remember that night at the Dorchester, and the Scots lassie with the fog-daubed nostrils who joined them half-way through dinner!

On another of those Ally Pally dates I was on the same bill with the Serenading Twins, and one of them told me a hair-raising tale, which haunted me for many a long day afterwards.

She'd fallen in love with and married an American GI during the war, and afterwards, like thousands of other English girls, she'd joined her GI in the States. They had a lovely flat in New York, and, with the baby which came along shortly afterwards, were as happy as birds in their nest. His work took him out at very odd hours, mostly at night, and sometimes even all through the night, and she was never too clear what it was he did. She thought it was something to do with investments or real estate, which necessitated his seeing out-of-town clients at out-of-hours meetings. She didn't mind not being able to go out with him in the evenings, for he was home a lot during the day, and shared in the pleasure of being with the baby more than most working fathers.

All was going merry as a marriage bell, and whatever it was he did brought in rich rewards, for theirs was a very expensive apartment, and they had a large car, and she had only to express a wish for anything and it was hers. And then one night the door-bell rang, and when her husband went to open it four tough-looking policemen were standing there. Before he could reach for his gun, they had pinned him down. And only then did she learn that he was one of the most wanted men in America. One of the Public Enemies in fact, with a number all his own, somewhere a little down the line from Al Capone! This charming man with whom she'd shared her life was a gangster. And she hadn't suspected a thing.

And now that she knew, all sorts of little things fell into place and made sense. How could she have been so blind? She looked at the baby and felt sick for his future and decided that she must go back to England and make a new life for herself, and for her child. And that was when I met her, and she was beginning to build her career all over again. I discovered that her brother had been on the bill with me at Glasgow Empire, or rather that I had been on the bill with him! And here I was, meeting his sister on TV. It made me realize that on a certain level the world of show business is like a private club, where it doesn't take too long to get to know all the members.

Apart from being welcomed by so many TV producers to join their shows, I was also always being asked to do night-club and cabaret work. This I utterly refused to do. 'I'm not the type,' I'd say desperately. 'I'm not sophisticated enough, and, besides, I haven't got a night-club act.' Those who wanted me to appear didn't care whether or not I died of fright because I knew I didn't fit that scene, they just wanted to be able to advertise that 'Tattie of ITMA' would be appearing, so that curiosity would bring the audiences in. But I'd have been the one who had to face them, and I knew I was wrong for this sort of work. It wasn't lack of courage, it was clear common sense.

But one day Ted Kavanagh called me in to see him at his

office and asked if I would, as a personal favour, appear at a 'smokers' concert' to be held on the top floor of Lyons in Coventry Street about 10.30 p.m. the following week. The audience would be entirely male, it didn't matter what I did, but they were dying to see me, and he had promised I'd come along and do a fifteen minutes' spot! He brushed aside my fears, said this wasn't an ordinary night-club engagement, but a simple night out for the boys, and that it was time I added this sort of experience to my repertoire.

I've always hated work which started at around my bedtime, and my teeth were chattering with nerves as I dressed in my Guide uniform behind screens, and tried to shut out the sound of maudlin laughter and chatter out there in that vast room. The haze of smoke was so dense it almost choked me, and the thought of trying to entertain that roomful of half-tight men nearly frightened me out of my wits. When I was dressed, I stepped aside to let a young man go behind the screens to change, and to check his props, of which there seemed to be quite a few. 'Good luck,' he whispered when the compère announced 'Your own, your very own Tattie!' and the next minute I was facing them and warbling 'Please, Captain, I've swallowed my whistle'.

They didn't want to hear a word of it. 'Good old Tattie,' they shouted. 'How's Tommy Handley?'

Completely inexperienced in the repartee of the music hall, I murmured ineptly, 'He's fine!' This brought the house down. All they wanted was to hear my voice and to check that I really was Scots, it seemed. So we indulged in a bit of question and answer, and I finished up with 'I belong to Glasgow', feeling more dead than alive, and vowing I'd *never* as long as I lived be conned into doing another late-night show. And the applause and cheers did nothing to make me change my mind.

The young chap went on and I thought he was great, but he played to almost stony silence. Not a laugh. Not a titter. He worked like a demon, and came off to polite applause. 'Oh, Molly,' he said, 'that was *awful*. Not a laugh! I died the death.'

I felt so angry with that stupid audience, and so sorry for him. 'Don't bother your head about *them*,' I said, forgetting I'd been terrified of them myself a short half-hour earlier, 'they're drunk. They only applauded me because I'm a name to them from ITMA. My performance was terrible compared with yours. Yours is a *real* act.' I always had the greatest admiration and respect for a well-thought-out variety act, which I knew I did not possess myself. 'Tell me your name,' I said, 'for I want to recognize it when I see it up in lights one day, which I am sure it will be, when you are a great star.'

He laughed. 'Harry Secombe,' he said, 'Harry Secombe.' 'I won't forget,' I replied.

I like to think I shared a wee bit of my grannie's second sight that night, and recognized star quality when I saw it, and wasn't just softening the sickening disappointment felt by an unknown young man whose brilliant comedy had meant nothing to this unresponsive audience. It had been like casting pearls before swine.

The next time I met him was on a film set. I had been asked to play maidservant to Freddie Frinton, with Harry and Michael Bentine playing a couple of wanderers who come to our door looking for a hand-out. We had the usual film start of around 7.30 a.m., which meant, as far as I was concerned, being out of bed before 6 a.m. to get to the studio before seven, but in spite of everyone's sleepy condition, Harry made us all laugh so much with his antics and his clowning that we were utterly exhausted by the time the cameras were ready to 'shoot'. Sleep was banished in gales of laughter, but even he had to lie down flat on the floor to recover, so hilarious and riotous was the fun.

He's a natural clown, a most lovable man, with a spontaneous and infectious sense of fun.

It was in this film I heard him sing seriously for the first time, an impressive operatic piece, and I was so carried away I cried out afterwards, 'Harry, you *must* study singing properly, and concentrate on it, for you have a magnificent voice.' The cheek of me, as if the man didn't know his own talent. But I do know he was terribly torn between opera and comedy at that time, and it didn't seem possible to combine the two successfully. One of my secret wishes, if ever a good fairy godmother had come along with a choice for me, had always been to choose the gift of a really beautiful singing voice, and I couldn't bear the thought that the possessor of a voice like Harry's might waste such a gift because of the clash with his other great talent for comedy. So I was bold enough to speak, and because he realized I was sincere he told me of his dilemma – opera or comedy? Which was it to be? And, of course, we all know he did manage to combine both splendid talents, and we the public are the richer for it.

My neighbours are always impressed to see a Christmas card from Harry Secombe on the mantelpiece display. 'How is it you know him so well, then?' they ask me, puzzled. And I smile and see again a fairly slight young man ducking behind screens as I walked out to a smoke-filled room, and I murmur, 'Well, you see I knew him when he was just starting.'

And I sometimes wonder if any of that unresponsive audience later recognized in the top star for whom they maybe queued at the London Palladium, the young man whom they had dismissed so indifferently in Lyons many years before.

3

When the decision was taken to part with Tony Francis (Reg Raspberry) from the ITMA cast it was necessary to bring in another artist to bring us up to strength. Among those auditioned was Joan Harben, sister of Philip, who was later to have all our mouths watering with his delicious TV cookery, and daughter of famous West End actress Mary Jerrold. I was most impressed, remembering my own amateur approach, when Joan told me later that she'd heard through the grape-vine of these auditions. (I didn't even know what a grape-vine was, as applied to inside information!) Because she wasn't a radio performer, but worked mostly on the West End stage, which also kept her husband Clive Morton busy, she adopted a truly professional attitude and had Reginald (Tony) Beckwith write her a specially commissioned audition script. I was quite staggered by this esoteric awareness – fancy knowing just where to go to find a man who would write the correct sort of material, and fancy even knowing that poor Tony Francis wasn't having his six weeks' contract renewed, especially when she wasn't even in the swim of radio work!

Such concentration deserved success, and it was duly rewarded. The piece Tony wrote for her was based on her own 'daily', who would arrive, unburden herself of all her aches and pains and grumbles, delivered in a lugubrious toneless voice, and at the end, to Joan's brisk 'I don't know how you manage,' she would invariably reply 'It's being so cheerful as keeps me going.'

And as soon as they heard those words, Ted Kavanagh and Francis Worsley knew they'd found their replacement. And Mona Lott was born. In spite of the difference in our ages, we got on with one another like a house afire, and were joyous companions from the word go. I never felt I was too young or gauche with her, as I often did with others. With the uncertainty of theatre employment, Joan hadn't been used to the security of a regular salary such as ITMA provided, with all its repeats both at home and abroad, any more than I had since entering the hazardous world of show business, and we both hugged ourselves with delight over our good fortune. She had a wonderful sense of humour, and although not pretty-pretty in the conventional sense of the word, had an elegant pale grace which I found very attractive. When we had to stay away from London after a charity show which wouldn't allow us to return the same night, she and I always shared a room, from choice, and found that we also shared a preference for well-cared-for healthy skin and well-brushed hair, and were like a couple of schoolgirls in the dorm, telling one another virtuously that too much make-up was a ruination of skin texture, and that we preferred to use just enough to enhance our appearance, but not so much that we were a ghastly contrast when it was all removed. It never occurred to us that we were being smug when we surveyed our bedtime pale clean faces so approvingly! We were just pleased we'd followed our mothers' golden rules, and were rewarded with skins which manifested not the smallest pimple or roughness. One could be completely honest with Joan, without the slightest fear of misunderstanding, a rapport I didn't always feel with people south of the border, whose ways were very different from mine.

The public adored her, and Mona Lott was an instant favourite, and 'It's being so cheerful as keeps me going' was heard everywhere, on the Tube, in the buses and in the pubs. Even as I write this, twenty-five years later, a headline in today's paper carries the words 'IT'S BEING SO CHEERFUL AS KEEPS US GOING', referring to strike-suffering London, and I wonder how many of those who read the headline realized it came from ITMA and, more particularly, from Joan Harben's char?

In spite of her understated appearance, for she never *looked* like an actress, with her delicate skin, soft dark straight hair and subdued clothes, she had a terrific awareness of the value of publicity and was always thinking up schemes to get her name and photograph into the newspapers. I was fascinated to think one could manufacture such events, for I thought the newspapers found the personality, not the other way round. Joan, who had been steeped in theatre all her life, both her parents having been top-liners for years, knew otherwise. For, of course, every theatre has a pub-licity manager, who sees to it that all shows are brought to the public notice via gossip, coincidental happenings, accidents to the cast, weddings, anniversaries, anything which will keep the show in the news and stimulate public interest. This was Joan's world, and she was very familiar with all its workings.

She and Tony Beckwith were just about to launch a great publicity scheme when I quite unwittingly knocked her and everyone else off the front page for an entire week!

It was a bitterly cold January and February, and we were having yet another miners' dispute. Fuel cuts were ordered by the Government, and anyone who wanted to save coal and electricity at home and decided to go to a theatre or cinema found when they got there they had merely ex-changed the misery of shivering before their own depleted firesides, to quaking with cold in unheated theatres and picture-houses. I travelled in icy trains, and took to wearing my gardening trousers for the journeys between Glasgow and London, preferring warmth to fashion, for in those days trousers for females were far from being *haute couture*. Especially mine, which had helped me 'dig for victory' and bore the scars to prove it! In fact, Rose, my sister-in-law, said that if somebody as thin as I could look so ungainly in trousers, she for one would never be seen dead in them. Also, as I normally went straight from Euston to Clapham to see to my mail, clothes and shopping before the afternoon rehearsal, I just kept my hair up in kirby-pinned curls under a scarf-cum-turban for the early-morning return to my digs, so that I'd be sure of well-set coiffure for later-in-the-day rehearsals in the West End.

So I was not exactly Miss Clapham of 1947 when I stepped off the train one bitterly cold morning in February and observed with some surprise that the platform was alive with cameras and newsmen. I looked round to see which famous film star might be emerging from the first-class coaches, and for a wild moment thought it might even be Garbo, who maybe had attempted to 'be alone' in my country for a change.

I was astounded to find all the newsmen, following a jerked head and a 'That's her' from the guard, pouncing on *me*. 'What's happened?' I cried. 'What is it? Has Korda awarded me a £10,000 contract?' I had a profound belief it was only a matter of time before I was 'discovered' by this fairy godfather of the silver screen, and film stardom was just round the corner.

The newsmen stopped dead. 'Do you mean to say you haven't heard the news?' they asked, delighted that this was to be an even better story than they'd thought. They were clearly to be the *first* to tell me all. 'You were mentioned in

Parliament last night,' they said unexpectedly. 'In Parliament!' I repeated, feeling it a terrible let-down after my dreams of Korda, and yet in a way even more improbable. In the midst of a fuel crisis what on earth could the Prime Minister and Members of Parliament find to talk about which would include me? And, of course, this was the point of all the excitement on the part of the newspapers. They were absolutely ecstatic to find something which would take the public mind off coal-less grates, cold houses and places of entertainment, and dreary headlines.

It appeared that the previous night, during a debate in the House, Mrs Jean Mann, MP for Coatbridge, had stated that in ITMA she saw the greatest insult to Scotland. This programme had a Scots girl who was supposed to be falling off her head for that little twerp Tommy Handley. She added for good measure that in her generation no Scotswoman would have looked at such a twerp twice!

If she had attacked the Throne itself she couldn't have caused a greater sensation. And here was every newspaper in London demanding to know my instant reactions. 'What had I to say?' 'Did I think she had a point?' 'What did I think of Tommy Handley?' Their pencils scribbled away as I told them I thought it was terribly funny. That I couldn't imagine anyone looking at Tommy's humour from a sex angle. That you couldn't judge a sausage from its skin, and I found him a delight to work with. That I didn't know where Mrs Mann's Scottish sense of humour had gone, because from the dozens of letters I'd received everybody took my chasing after Tommy as a great joke. Then to my dismay a battery of press cameras were turned on me and it was then I remembered my trousers. 'Oh *don't* get my gardening trousers in the picture,' I implored. What Sandy would say if he saw me in the newspapers with those old corduroys I didn't dare to think. And my hair up in pins under my turban, which he hated! It was obvious that I'd just come off a sleeper. Och, what a sight I must look. But the photographers weren't going to be robbed of their pictures and banged off flashlights by the dozen before speeding away back to the dark-rooms of their newspaper offices.

At last the reporters let me go, and when I reached my room in Clapham the telephone was ringing shrilly. Mrs Parker put her head round her kitchen door. 'I don't know what's going on,' she said crossly, 'but I've been up those stairs a dozen times already, and it's not even nine o'clock, answering that telephone of yours. You've to ring . . .' and she reeled off a string of magazines and weeklies who wanted me to call them back.

This story would have been news at any time, of course, but just then in the midst of icy misery it was manna from heaven, and everyone wanted to get in on the act. The phone never stopped ringing. The moment I'd dealt with one magazine, the receiver had barely been put back when the bell shrilled out again. I couldn't even get a cup of tea. It never occurred to me to leave it off the hook. Francis Worsley rang, delighted with all this heaven-sent publicity. 'Come an hour earlier to rehearsal, Molly,' he said, 'we've called a press conference, with photographers.'

'Oh gosh,' I said, 'I hope I'll have time to eat something first, because I can get no peace here even to boil a kettle.'

He laughed callously. 'Never mind food at a time like this,' he said, 'this is worth ten thousand pounds in publicity, and we want you for press photographs.'

On the way to the Paris the billboards carried the words 'Tattie answers Mrs Mann'. My stomach gave a twinge of nervous excitement. Fancy them thinking it important enough to put it on the *Bills*! In Glasgow, Rangers would have to have scored ten goals to rate such publicity, or the rents would have to have doubled overnight! Biting my lips nervously and wondering what on earth I'd said to all those newsmen at the station, I bought a couple of newspapers when I got off the bus. Oh good! Most of the pictures showed head and shoulders only, with never a sign of the tattered breeks. One showed me with hands in pockets, carrying my little straw bag, travel rug over my arm. I was glad I'd travelled in my best coat, a pale mustard tweed with nutria collar; I'd forgotten I had it on in my despair over the trousers. And the turban actually looked not bad – only *I* knew that underneath my hair was in its bedtime grips. Every word I had uttered had been quoted. There were paragraphs and paragraphs – just as if I were a politician myself. It didn't seem possible that without any action on my part to contrive this, I'd be the talk of Britain. I was utterly bewildered by the intensity of the interest and the reaction, and agreed with my mother's later assessment, 'Ah don't know whit that wumman Mann got so excited aboot,' she said, 'for a' ye have to say, naebody would know ye were *in* the programme.'

At the Paris, Tommy was walking about, pipe clenched in his teeth, grinning with delight. The photographers were moving things around to make suitable backgrounds for their pictures. I was pictured sitting on Tommy's knee, fending off Miss Hotchkiss (Diana Morrison). Emerging from a supposed car, with Tommy gallantly offering me an umbrella and saying, 'Wot, Tattie? No Mackintosh?' Hiding with Tommy inside our little cubicle which was fronted by our famous door, whose slam had a character all its own. Trying to embrace Tommy, with him backing away in terror. And so on. And so on.

The script was re-written, and when we went on the air that Thursday at 8.30 p.m. the excitement in the Paris was electric. The studio fairly crackled with anticipation. The audience and the listening public knew Ted Kavanagh would have a bonanza, and he did. Instead of opening with the usual 'It's that man again', we started with 'It's that twerp again', which had the audience in a roar. Then he said he was going to sing a new song from the show 'The Squeak in Westminster', entitled 'Mrs Mann, you've had a busy day'. 'And if you're listening, Mrs Mann, I'm in Room 504 – knock twice and ask for Twerpy.' Gag after gag was adjusted to suit the situation, and millions of people forgot they were cold, listening to that cocky voice cheeking back at poor Mrs Mann, who had no idea what an avalanche she'd started when she threw that tiny pebble in the pool of the Parliamentary debate.

The papers played it for all it was worth for a week. Pocket cartoons showed two sophisticated ladies exchanging gossip. 'Did you hear? ITMA's been Mann-handled'. The main cartoon in the *Standard* showed me wooing Mr Attlee, the Prime Minister, instead of Tommy Handley. The fuel crisis was well and truly swiped, and the whole nation, it seemed, was saying 'It's being so cheerful as keeps us going'.

And I was invited to the House of Commons by Mrs Mann, to listen to the debate on conscription! She rang me up one day and asked me to take lunch with her there, for being such a sport about the whole thing. She had felt the press had taken her remarks very seriously, and had felt entitled to be able to poke fun. Anyway, she said, Mrs Handley's boy wasn't everybody's cup of tea and she couldn't stomach so many girls falling for him!

Personally, after meeting this delightful little woman, I felt she had engineered the whole thing just to take the pressure off the Government because of the fuel crisis. And succeeded beyond her wildest dreams, I'd say.

I was thrilled to dine in the Parliamentary dining room,

and to be taken up to the gallery afterwards to listen to the debate. The members all looked so different from their newspaper photographs, more ordinary somehow, for, of course, we only ever saw them during times of crisis when they were being interviewed, or making grave statements of policy. Now they were about their everyday business and much more casual than I could have believed. I'd been peering down at them for a good ten minutes, trying to identify them from their photographs, when a pair of legs stretched out to reach the Dispatch Box on the table in front of him caught my attention. Fancy sitting with his feet up there, I thought indignantly, remembering the numerous times we'd been told at home by my mother and grannie to 'keep your feet *doon* and don't scuff the furniture'. And here was a fully grown MP in the House of Commons sitting with his feet on a table. I looked closer, and my heart gave a lurch. The legs belonged to my hero, Winston Churchill! Of course! The Opposition Front Bench. I opened my eyes as wide as possible to take in his unexpectedly pink face, his pale hair, and the famous chin sunk into his chest. I was in the same building as the man who had saved us all from the thraldom of Hitler. I wanted to stand up and cheer, but knew I'd be thrown out, so just sat quietly gazing at him until the debate ended. And I remembered that it was all part of the tradition of the House that famous front-benchers could put their feet up on that table, and blushed to think I'd dared criticize him in my ignorance. Oh, it was an unforgettable afternoon, and I was only there because I was in ITMA.

I think Mrs Mann would have loved to have met Tommy and to have been invited to the show, but the meeting never took place. Francis Worsley, with a shrewd assessment of the situation, decided we'd had every drop of publicity that could possibly be milked out of it, and wanted no more time wasted on such politenesses. Each week brought its hard demands for needle-sharp scripts, and the three principals sweated over them as though they were writing *Hamlet*. Faces tense and white, a line was changed here and there until all was perfect.

In the Kavanagh 'training stable', as his office came to be known, were two possible future comedy writers whom he was nursing along in the hope that at some later date they would be fully fledged experts like himself. Ted had a keen eye for talent, and I used to watch those two enormously tall thin chaps bent over their desks scribbling a word here, a sentence there, then staring into space with worried frowns. They reminded me of storks with their long legs, and it was always a surprise to find such quiet voices coming from such a long way above my head. I wondered how Ted could know if his investment would pay off, for he was paying them a salary while they were studying their craft. But he didn't go far wrong with those two! They were, of course, Frank Muir and Denis Norden, creators of *Take It from Here* scripts and many others, whose brilliance later had all Britain chuckling. Afterwards they went into TV where I worked with them myself; and on radio, as I write, they still delight us with *My Word* and *My Music*. Even in those ITMA days, when I used to see them in the Kavanagh office, Denis had the same halting style of telling a story, and one just had to hang on to his every word, for the end was always worth waiting for. But in that era of the quick gag I'd never have imagined this style would become such a riotous success when he became a performer himself. By remaining true to his own pace and timing, he brought the rest of us to see it was hilarious, and educated our ear to his particular brand of comedy. Frank hardly spoke a word in the office. Just loomed up out of his chair to reach out a hand for some more paper, or a whispered consultation with Denis or Mary Harris, the executive I was usually visiting, and with a shy smile loped back to his desk again. Now look at him! One of the most authoritative voices in the world of comedy! I reckon if it had been race-horses Kavanagh had been training, he'd have won the Derby and the Grand National nae bother, with such an eye for picking winners.

Ted's wife Agnes was a Scot, like myself, and I remember after one party given by Lind Joyce, our resident singer in ITMA, Agnes and I entertained the others with our impromptu sword dance, executed after a long delicious 'fruit' drink called a John Collins, which turned out to contain a large proportion of gin! Ted wasn't sure who was leading who astray, and was astounded to see his douce Agnes facing up to me, arms held high, and toes twinkling nimbly over and across the fire-irons which masqueraded as our swords.

It was only when I thirstily held out my glass for a second helping of that lovely drink with the fruit and mint floating so tantalizingly on top that I was gently deflected towards the orange juice and advised that one John Collins was sufficient for a Rechabite like me! No wonder they say the devil can come in many guises, for I'd never have believed that anything which tasted so innocuous contained hard liquor. With memories of the Savoy, I needed no further persuasion to eschew treacherous John Collins.

But Ted talked of that sword dance for years afterwards. He'd been married half a lifetime to his dear wee Agnes and hadn't known she had such hidden talent!

Another party was given for us at the Savile Club, of which some of our male stars were members. This exclusive club was near Savile Row and I was most interested to visit the famous street of tailors who dressed everyone from

Royalty down. Quiet and discreet, with lovely old buildings, it fairly took hold of my imagination, and once I'd discovered this lovely byway, I always walked through it to get to Aeolian Hall and Bond Street. I still do. Much of it has changed now, but it is still worth strolling through. The party was for ITMA's 250th performance, and although I'd only been with them a short time as a member of the present cast, I was included in the invitation. We went there after our show, and we had little savoury 'bites' and a huge cake with 250 in raised iced lettering, which Tommy cut, and we all received a slice to nibble with our champagne toast 'to the next 250'. I couldn't finish mine, with its rich marzipan, and greatly amused Ted Kavanagh by asking for a little paper bag to take it home. I wasn't going to leave that rich weddingy cake behind me – it would have been a terrible waste, and I hadn't tasted anything so delicious for years, and wanted to savour it on a more favourable occasion with a cup of tea, when I'd really appreciate it. I didn't care if they thought it very 'Scottish' of me. Years of being told 'think of the starving Europeans' had instilled in me a dread of wasted food, and I knew perfectly well they'd just have thrown my half-nibbled cake into the bin. So I risked their laughter, and fairly enjoyed it next day with my tea.

In spite of her supposed coolness about my part in the show, my mother took little coaxing to come back with me on one of my return journeys, so that she could see ITMA for herself. I felt she would enjoy the atmosphere, and maybe understand the importance of the programme if she saw the audience's enthusiasm, and, of course, meet all the famous cast. She was astounded at the queues winding round the Paris waiting for the hour to strike, and quite mesmerized by the size of the orchestra. I think she enjoyed Rae Jenkins and his music best of all, for her hearing wasn't ever good, but she adored music and dancing, and she was fascinated by the way we all moved back and forth from the mike as the script demanded.

'Aye,' she said afterwards, 'by jings I can see you could be a nervous wreck wi' a' thae lights, and that door banging, and a' thae folk clapping.' She never again hinted that it wasn't worth my while going back to London to play Tattie. But she certainly thought it was high time I bought myself a new bed, for she'd hardly slept a wink trying to avoid the lumps like turnips in the mattress. It was a terrible bed. But landladies were terrified to allow tenants to put furniture into 'furnished' rooms in case they would then regard them as 'unfurnished' and so be unable to be given notice to leave, if the landlady had any complaints about behaviour or anything else.

However, my mother's words emboldened me to try again. Maybe now I was 'somebody' in radio, Mrs Parker would trust me to buy a new bed, which I could share with Sandy with some degree of comfort when he came down, and surely give me better sleep when I was there on my own. To all previous suggestions of this sort, she had scurried away after saying she'd let me know later. Now I pinned her down. Supplies of all sorts of goods were getting easier, and I'd seen a very good three quarter-size bed in the furniture stores round the corner, which was as large as I could hope she would allow as a replacement for the worn-out old single one, and would seem blissfully roomy by comparison with the narrow bench I'd endured for more than a year. She hummed and ha'ed for a bit, but I stood my ground, and by the end of that week I had a new bed, and a new mattress, and the old one was consigned to the basement, to be lugged up again at some future date if ever I gave up my room. I was so glad my mother had put some steel into my backbone, and from then on was able to snuggle down with perfect comfort in my very own bed in my room high above the chimneys.

My mother was aghast at the disparity between the suave airs of the Londoners and the rubbish with which they furnished their homes or offices. I took her to have a hearing aid fitted, much against her will, I may say, for she was getting so deaf that my throat was strained to croaking point trying to make her hear what I was saying, and I simply couldn't afford this sort of punishment when I was in such an important radio show. To make her wear the instrument, I showed her the amount for which I'd made out the cheque, for I knew she abhorred waste and if nothing else would persuade her to wear the gadget, the thought of all that good money wasted would. When she'd recovered from the shock, she pursed her lips, looked all round the Harley Street surgery with critical eyes, and said, as she surveyed the specialist's chair with sagging upholstery, 'Well, ah hope the first thing he does wi' a' that money is buy a new chair for himsel'. That yin has the behind hingin' oot o' it. He must have been gey glad tae see you comin'.' Always a realist, my mother! I practically had hysterics, for the immaculate specialist was in the room by this time, and I only trusted he couldn't understand a word of her broad Scots.

And then almost before I knew it, we were coming up to the last performance, and singing the words of the final chorus, 'I go, I come back. In the autumn again I'll be here. I go, I come back, with a song and a smile, and a tear. For a little while we leave you, with a smile . . .' and then we went into the mike one at a time, and said our name, 'Tommy, Diana, Hugh, Fred, Lind, Deryck, Joan, Molly, Jack' . . . roll of drums . . . *'We go . . . we come back!'*

I could hardly sing for emotion. For I felt I just wouldn't be coming back. I had no reason for feeling like this. But my stomach, that wise part of my anatomy with the sixth sense, told me so. And when the newspapers wanted to know my holiday plans, for the lightest utterances of the ITMA cast were news, I told them truthfully that I was going home to do some belated spring cleaning, then Sandy and I were going on a walking holiday either in Cornwall or the Highlands. 'You'll be back in good time for September and the new series?' they asked me, laughingly. I said that my re-engagement on the programme wasn't automatic, and they quoted me in the press as being very canny, but said they would be very surprised if I were not in the team when the series came back.

Tommy, Ted and Francis, with Jack Train, went off to America for the summer, for the combined purpose of having a long relaxing holiday and taking a look at American humour with an eye to the next series.

We went off to Cornwall, and had a glorious fortnight walking all over that lovely county, and all was perfect but for that little nagging black doubt in my stomach. Anyway, Henry Hall rang and invited me to take part in his guest night in Glasgow Empire in a few weeks' time, and the thought of having to provide a variety script knocked all other anxieties out of my head, for now I would be judged as a professional, and not an amateur 'discovery', and I'd have to provide solid eighteen-carat material – or get the bird!

4

Henry Hall was a tremendous favourite in Glasgow, and was guaranteed to pack the Empire for every performance. I had never written a real variety script, and would have begged Ted Kavanagh to write this important one for me, but, of course, he was deep in the heart of America by this time, with Francis Worsley and Tommy, and there was nothing else for it but to have a stab at it myself.

I decided to incorporate both Tattie and Tattie's mother, and wrote a telephone conversation on the ITMA lines, but slanted to reflect Glasgow humour, and bringing in the shy Henry Hall to interrupt, just as Tommy Handley did in ITMA. I then worked in my impersonations, finishing up with Tommy Morgan, at Henry's request, and timed the whole thing to suit the slot I was to be allowed on the bill. Sandy and I went over and over the script, polishing and pruning, for he was even more nervous about this appearance than I was, as all his office colleagues intended being there, and it was one thing disappointing mere Londoners, but quite another setting myself up as an Aunt Sally for his office pals!

Out of the blue I was offered a song by an ex-electrician at the Glasgow Pavilion Theatre, Johnny Stevenson, written in collaboration with his friend Billy Graham, and called 'Hearts of Glasgow', and I knew I'd found my opening number. Johnny was a talented amateur song writer, and I was more than happy to introduce his song on my first appearance in Glasgow since becoming Tattie in ITMA.

So here I was with an opening number and an act, and as nervous as a cartload of monkeys, for the publicity machine had gone to work and all Glasgow knew that Molly Weir, the wee Glasgow lassie who had 'conquered London as Tattie', was returning to Glasgow to be Henry Hall's special guest at the Glasgow Empire. The gossip columns even announced that I'd written my own script, for I foolishly imparted this titbit when they'd asked if the script was from the Kavanagh office. Now if it was a flop, everybody would know exactly where to place the blame!

We rehearsed at the theatre on the Sunday, as usual, and Henry Hall was absolutely charming. I'd sent him Johnny Stevenson's song in advance, and he had had it scored for the orchestra, and it sounded quite marvellous to my ears. On the Monday we rehearsed the whole show, words, music, everything, and at lunchtime Sandy joined us and took us across the road to the YMCA canteen for lunch, as he was a member there. What Henry Hall thought of being asked to queue up for lunch in such a modest setting, I just don't know, and if he considered it less lush than his usual setting he gave no hint, and seemed thoroughly to enjoy being part of the Glasgow lunchtime scene. It never dawned on us till long afterwards, that it must have been unusual, to say the least, for a famous band-leader to have been invited to dine at the YMCA among the crowds teeming from the Glasgow offices. Mouths fell open in astonishment as diners took a second startled look at the famous face in their midst, and the normal lunchtime chatter was subdued to a low buzz of excited whispering as the news spread that Henry Hall himself was dining with 'the lads' of Glasgow, and was tucking into mince and tatties with the best of them.

Sandy took a photograph of Henry and me walking along Sauchiehall Street and rushed it down to the *Daily Record* and it appeared on the front page next day, under the caption 'Recognize them?' Sandy had been a photographer in the RAF and was (and still is) very skilled with the camera, and it was great fun to find my quiet husband entering into the spirit of the thing, and promoting a little publicity of his own!

For my Henry Hall guest appearance I wore the full white taffeta skirt of my wedding dress, topped with a white short-sleeved blouse with a pussy-cat bow, and over the blouse the little red tartan waistcoat I'd made from a piece of material given to brother Willie as a duster on his visit to one of the factories, too good to use for this purpose and brought home to me, and by some never-to-be-repeated magic transformed into the neatest little Scottish waistcoat the heart could desire. I have it to this day and I still don't know how I managed to make such a fine job of it, for I have never flattered myself I'd win any prizes in the dressmaker stakes. But just once I achieved sewing perfection, and it was good enough for the Glasgow Empire, for my outfit was voted by at least one critic as not only extremely attractive, but 'good-looking and lady-like'! By jove, that pleased my mother more than anything else.

The audiences were marvellous, and after the first-house nervousness of the Monday night, when I trembled for the fate of my home-made script, I enjoyed the rest of that week with possibly slightly less terror than I had anticipated. The notices were good, and Gracie Fields asked for Johnny's song for her next visit to Glasgow for a broadcast and an appearance at St Andrew's Hall, and when the song was published later that year it was Gracie's picture which appeared on the song sheet. But I was the one who introduced it to Glasgow audiences! And it had sounded good enough to intrigue the great Gracie, and put Johnny's name on the musical map.

On the last night, Saturday, I decided to go out for a snack between the houses instead of staying in my dressing room as I usually did. Sandy was coming to the second house, to savour the special flavour of a packed Saturday-night audience, and was coming straight from home, so I nipped along to a small tearoom nearby to enjoy a Glasgow pie and chips. Nobody counted the calories in post-war Britain, and it was great to find pies with real meat in them again. On the way up in the lift afterwards, I happened to glance at a newspaper one of the other passengers was reading. Across the page were the words, 'Rangers beaten 3-nil'. Suddenly I had an idea. 'Is Gerry Dawson Rangers' goalkeeper?' I asked. The man looked at me pityingly.

'Of course he is – the hale o' Glesca knows that.' 'Are you sure?' I persisted, for it was essential to the success of my idea that I made no mistake. He looked at me in exasperation and said, 'Hoo often dae I have to tell you?' and he thrust the paper under my nose. 'Therr it is in black an' white – Gerry Dawson let three goals through the day.' I was elated. It was a pity about the Rangers' supporters, but I had found my second encore for the Tommy Morgan impersonation. I always had an encore, and inevitably shouts for another, for Tommy was still the favourite voice for my audiences, and up till now I had had to shake my head imperceptibly at Henry Hall to signal 'No more encores', take my final bow and disappear. But not tonight.

The Empire was packed. It was standing room only. At the end of the second Morgan encore, the audience whistled, and cheered and called for more. Henry looked at me, baton raised to bring in the orchestra with my play-off music, but instead of the shake of the head, I smiled at him and nodded. He looked at me in surprise, and raised his eyebrows enquiringly. I nodded again, and he held the orchestra silent.

I walked to the microphone, my heart pounding like a sledge-hammer. There was nothing which could bring more riotous reaction than an up-to-the-minute topical gag, and nothing which could fall so abysmally flat than one which flopped. It was do or die. In Tommy Morgan's raucous tones I said tragically, 'Aw jings, ma coupon's burst. Ah think Gerry must have been dossin' this efternoon.' The theatre erupted. The roar might have been heard at Hampden. The topicality of such a pun coming from a girl sent them whistling, cheering, and slapping each other in delight. Henry was quite bewildered. 'What did you *say*?' he kept asking, under the noise. But I couldn't speak. At that moment I felt that Glasgow belonged to me, and the warm appreciation of a great Glasgow audience enveloped me in its affection. I think it was one of the happiest moments of my professional life. I had pleased my ain folk.

Afterwards, Sandy rushed round to the dressing room, almost speechless with pride that I had gone down so well. 'Who made up the football pun?' he asked. 'Naebody,' said I, reverting to Springburn repartee, 'I made it up masel'.'

He stared at me with some respect. 'But how did you know Gerry Dawson was Rangers' goalkeeper?' he demanded, 'You know nothing about football.'

'I saw it in a man's paper in the lift,' I told him.

'Well, you'll never make up a better one if you live to be a hundred.' He told me he had trembled with nerves for me when I came out to do the second encore, for he thought I couldn't possibly top the first one. But for that one performance a newspaper headline had given me the perfect finish, and I felt like going down on my knees, fasting, for opportunity being given to me to finish so triumphantly that lovely week with Henry Hall.

My mother's great moment came when she came back-stage to be introduced to him, for, of course, apart from his being a fine leader of a first-class band, he was also a gentleman. This in her eyes made him perfect. Her eyes sparkled with pure happiness when she shook his hand, but when he said she must be proud of me, she tossed me a quizzical look and merely answered, 'It's a wonder she disnae drap deid wi' a' the excitement.' To have said she was proud of one of her own weans would have smacked of showing off in my mother's eyes, and she had no intention of allowing me to get a swelled head with any mention of pride in me – not her! But I think she maybe had a small suspicion that I must have something to offer audiences if the great and gentlemanly Henry Hall could use me in his show.

After all this heady excitement it was another parting for us because I was due in London to do a radio series called *The Waitress, the Porter and the Upstairs Maid*, the one and only radio series for which I provided story-outline and idea. I had taken my brain-child along to Ted Kavanagh towards the end of the ITMA series and he liked it and had one of the senior script-writers, Rodney Hobson, discuss it with me fully and turn it into a six-part series, with an option for another six if it clicked with the public. The stories were fairly simple, but with good opportunities for comedy and singing. I was the waitress, and Irene Prador, the sister of Lilli Palmer, played the upstairs maid, and each week we battled for the affections of the porter, played by Clarence Wright, an ex-ITMA actor. It was all set within the hotel where we worked, and we had a different plot-line each week. One episode concerned itself with a hotel

63

thief, who, of course, was spotted and caught by us. Another had an espionage theme. A third found us involved with an American lady seeking evidence for a divorce, a fourth with money going missing and all of us under suspicion, a fifth with a guest who took a fancy to the porter and allowed Irene and me to gang up together against her, our rivalry forgotten for once. And the last one had us running the hotel on our own, because the manager collapsed with appendicitis. All simple story-lines, but very lively and fast, and the songs and duets were worked in to fit the situations. Joan Clark produced, and the whole thing went down very well with the public. But it was high summer, BBC staff changes were taking place, and in spite of our good ratings the new brooms swept us right out of the winter schedules, and our contracts weren't renewed. But it had been the greatest fun to do, and for me personally a great morale-booster to have my ideas translated so successfully into an entertaining radio series, for I felt I would need such comfort against the days ahead.

I was right. Not the pricking of my thumbs, but the twitching of my stomach had warned me of coming disappointment, so I was able to read the letter from Francis Worsley with almost a feeling of relief at knowing the worst. It was the problem of fitting the Scottish dialect and background into such an English show as ITMA which was the difficulty for the writers, and, reluctantly, he would have to tell me that he could not include me in the ITMA cast for the forthcoming series.

Well, if the press had had a field day when I joined the cast, they had another one now that I'd got the chop. Oh, with kindness and charm, but the chop nevertheless. At such a moment, I realized I had had the greatest good fortune to have been brought up in a background where children weren't spoilt. Grannie and my mother made us realize life was hard, and we must be prepared in every way to face it. That sort of attitude is a bulwark against anything life has to offer in the way of blows and disappointments. Especially when the blows must be taken in the full blazing spotlight of the national press.

The banner headlines met me everywhere. 'HATTIE REPLACES TATTIE' – for the newcomer was the splendid Hattie Jacques, at that time quite unknown on radio, but a tower of strength at the Players Theatre where, strangely enough, I later worked myself. 'TOMMY LOSES A GIRL FRIEND.' 'CURTAINS FOR TATTIE.' 'ITMA TEAM IS CHANGED – AND TATTIE GOES.' 'AN ITMA ADIEU.' 'TATTIE SAYS GOODBYE TO ITMA.' And reams of comments from everyone. From Ted Kavanagh, 'All of us, particularly Tommy Handley, are sorry to lose Molly. Her fan mail was proof of her popularity.' From Francis Worsley, 'Dialect is something which can be overdone. There is nothing personal about this decision, and we are sorry to see Molly go.' The papers rushed to the defence: 'Hattie Jacques is coming in to replace little Molly Weir, who prattled so nicely as Tattie. This should increase Francis Worsley's post-bag from Scotland!' 'ITMA comes back, but alas without little Molly Weir, the Scots girl who aroused the ire of Mrs Jean Mann, MP', and so on, and so on. Never-ending, and constantly probing to see if there had been a rift or if I was upset, but I blandly quoted Francis and said to one and all that he had decided to cut out the Scottish element. That he was genuinely sorry, I was sure, and so was I. And there they had to leave it.

But before the news broke, and while I was still in the team, I had an invitation to appear in *In Town Tonight*, which went out live each Saturday and featured celebrities in the news. I was thrilled beyond words to be asked to come along and be interviewed on this famous radio show, and caught my breath in wonder when I saw who the others were. The lovely Jean Simmons, then a young woman with all the bloom of dazzling youth, who had just made a big hit in films. It had only been supposed to be a small part, but when she sang 'Let him go, let him tarry', every critic predicted stardom, and *In Town Tonight* wanted to know all about her. There was a lady from occupied Greece, who had hidden blanket material in her loft, so that when liberation came she could pin the coloured pieces together and wave her home-made Union Jack out of the window within minutes of hearing that the war was over. She had a thrilling tale to tell of cunningly concealed radio sets, and death risked to listen to ITMA and the BBC news. I was to be asked about what it was like to be in ITMA. In the middle of discussions the door opened, and with swift steps in strode a startlingly handsome figure of a man. Dark blue coat, snowy silk scarf thrown round his neck, thick dark hair and splendid eyes. I gasped as I recognized Ivor Novello. He had come hot-foot from his matinée, and was to do his interview before the evening curtain. It was a dazzling moment for me, to be embraced in that wide sweet smile, and my mother had to hear a description of everything about him, and every last syllable of the interview, which she couldn't hear herself because of her deafness, and she sighed with pure rapture and closed her eyes and declared she could see it all just as if she had been there. In fact it was better than being there herself, for she'd have been too overawed to have taken it all in, whereas sitting in her own wee kitchen nothing disturbed her absorption of the word-picture I painted. I don't think she could have been more delighted if I had shared an interview with the Queen of England, for she adored Ivor Novello and felt some of the glory of the meeting had rubbed off on her.

But there was one terrible thing which happened during my year in ITMA of which I never breathed a word for years either to Sandy or to my mother, because I knew full well if they had the slightest idea I could be exposed to such danger they would never have let me return to London.

Mary, my friend from the factory days of wartime, had moved to Bournemouth to see if the gentler temperatures there would be kinder to her health, for she had an asthmatic condition, and she had found an excellent job, and a happy background for her living quarters in a church hostel. During a spell of glorious weather I decided that instead of staying in London for my five days between ITMA recordings and my next trip to Glasgow, I'd go down to Mary and renew our wartime friendship. I knew she'd be at work during the day, but I would be perfectly happy on the beach, for I've always loved the sea, and it would be like a little extra holiday. She found a room for me at the hostel, and it made an interesting change for me to have to stand up and sing a hymn with the girls before we sat down to a meal, which, of course, was always preceded by grace. On the first occasion, not knowing the routine, I was covered in confusion at finding myself the only person in the room sitting down in front of my plate, with everyone else poised to break into a hymn! I never felt such a heathen in my life.

Rationing was still severe, and fresh milk at a premium, and the girls had made the discovery that they could buy tins of dried milk for pregnant mums at the local chemist, which they purchased on a rota system, so that all shared the cost of the bedtime cocoa or other hot drink. The first time I heard one aged spinster remark to another, 'It's your turn to supply Radiant Motherhood,' I thought she was requesting a dramatic recitation. But it was the maternity dried milk she was describing, which was for their bedtime feasts and not for building the bonnie babies for which it was intended! What made me laugh most of all was the thought of this gentle deception practised within the sacred confines of the church hostel, where there was such pressing need for something nourishing to supplement the meagre diet, that nobody had the slightest sense of guilt.

It was a lovely few days, one sunny day following another, and I spent all my time in the sea, and sunbathing on the beach, reading and drowsing and walking, and relishing the complete contrast of this 'all girls together' life, which made a hilarious change from my solitary room in London and my busy housewife's life in Glasgow. On the last day, for I had to get back to London on the Tuesday evening, to be ready for my Wednesday rehearsal, I left my bag packed, all ready to leave when Mary got home from work, so she could wave me off at the station.

I lay on the beach all afternoon, glad I hadn't the desire or the need to compete for the lads' attention with all the summery girls in their holiday clothes, achieved with goodness knew what sacrifices of precious clothing coupons. Having nobody to impress I was happily content with my pre-war cotton dirndl, now a bit faded and out of fashion, and indifferent to the fact that my face was peeling with all the hot sun, and my hair sorely in need of a conditioning shampoo after days of sea and sun-bathing. I intended washing it when I got home to the digs, and my rosy salty cheeks would soon cool down once I was away from the sea.

I looked at my watch and decided I'd just have time for tea before I collected my luggage and met Mary, or I'd be starving by the time I got to Clapham. I walked smartly to the big store in town, which had a tea room and restaurant, and to my dismay saw they were already queuing for dinner, although it wasn't yet five o'clock, and dinners didn't start till six. Food shortages made it imperative to get a table anywhere in good time, for when the food ran out, it ran out, and in many places there could be no more than one sitting even if it were a public restaurant.

They had obviously decided to finish the afternoon teas early, for the restaurant was practically empty. I knew I'd never find anything anywhere else so late, so I decided to appeal to the sympathy of the waitress who was disappearing through a near door. I sped to the top of the queue and into the restaurant, calling to the queue, 'It's just tea I'm looking for,' in case there would be a riot at my rushing ahead of them, and caught the waitress. I explained that I had to catch a train for London, there would be no dining car, and I'd had nothing since lunchtime, and I whispered the magic name of ITMA. That did the trick. 'Sit down at that table there,' she said, 'and don't let anybody else see you, for I don't want any more teas so late in the day, before the dinner queues come in.' Breathing sighs of gratitude, I sat down, and said that whatever she could give me would be fine. Tea and some toast, and a bun if there was one going. I gazed out of the opposite window, determined to catch nobody's eye in case I'd be put out.

Suddenly footsteps sounded nearby, the chair beside mine was pulled back, and someone sat down beside me. My heart sank. If my example was going to be followed by other people demanding tea, we'd all be turned out, and by this time, when my lips were practically savouring the thirst-quenching brew, I felt I'd run amok if the cup were dashed from my lips now.

I gave the man beside me a baleful glare, and looked away. 'The cheek of him,' I thought, 'and to sit down right next to me when every single table in the room is empty.'

'Good evening,' he said. I was astounded at his temerity after the look I'd given him. I didn't reply. 'Good evening,' he said again, 'are you down here on holiday?'

'No,' I said.

'Oh,' he said, not one bit put out, 'do you live here then?'

'No,' I said again.

'Perhaps you just work here, then?' he asked, as smoothly and charmingly as though I were giving him every encouragement to talk.

'I am merely visiting a friend,' I replied as civilly as I could bring myself to say the words, 'and I am waiting for tea because I am going for the London train. I only hope that your presence won't prevent my getting it, because teas are finished.'

'I see,' he said. 'Well, it doesn't matter if I don't get tea. I just thought I'd like some, if there was any going. What are you doing tonight?' he added. I couldn't believe my ears. Bournemouth was full of pretty girls, all dressed to kill, and this man was asking me, in my tattered old cotton dress, what I was doing tonight! It didn't make sense. Unless he had a penchant for sunburned peeling noses and salt-filled hair, of course!

'I am going to London tonight,' I said in some irritation. 'I already told you.'

'Can't you put it off?' he asked.

'No,' I said through clenched teeth, wondering where my tea was, 'I can't.'

Then he said, 'I work for the BBC.'

I had such a strong conviction that he was trying to impress me that for the first time I swung right round in my seat and faced him. He had thick fair wavy hair, and was rather well dressed, but the most noticeable thing about him were his eyes – blue, and shining, and filled with a curious excitement. He was in fact such an obvious choice for a holiday pick-up for all those lovely girls in search of a little seaside romance that I couldn't for the life of me think why he was alone and bothering with a sight like me.

'Oh, you work for the BBC, do you?' I said with a touch of scornful disbelief. And then, very deliberately, staring him straight in the face, 'So do I. What is your name?'

He looked about him, thrown off balance for a second. Then, as his eye caught the name above the dais where the orchestra played at various times during the day, 'That's my name,' and he pointed to the surname of the restaurant band.

'You mean, it's *your* orchestra which plays here?' I asked him.

'No, no,' he smiled, 'I mean my name is the same as his.'

Now it was a single name, very fanciful, like Manicini – not exactly ordinary like Johnson, or Stapleton, or Black, and I didn't believe for a second that it was his name at all. I gave him one look of total scorn and turned to my tea, which had by now arrived. The girl refused to serve any more teas at first and I thought he'd have to leave, but he persuaded her that he wanted nothing to eat, just a pot of tea would do so she vanished to do his bidding.

As I ate my toast, slightly amazed to discover I had acquired such a talent for conveying that the man was lying in his teeth, he pursued the topic of seeing me later that night. He had a hide like a rhinocerous, I decided. Maybe he had such success with women as a rule that it was now a point of honour to make this tatty female succumb to his charm. 'Won't you change your mind about going back to London tonight?' he pressed. 'You could surely get an early train tomorrow morning.'

It was really almost laughable. Fancy anybody trying to talk me out of getting back to wash my hair and get my clothes organized for the next day's rehearsals for a show, my apearance in which was the sole reason for my being in the south at all.

I finished my toast, drank my tea, paid my bill and said, 'I'm sorry, but I'm off for my train now. I'm sure you'll find somebody else to amuse you this evening.'

When I met Mary I said laughingly, 'Well, hen, I nearly got a "click" tonight' (our Glasgow name for a casual pick-up), 'worn dress and all, he seemed to think I was the bee's knees.'

'My,' said Mary, 'and here's all of us girls in the church hostel living like nuns, and not a beau in sight!'

Next day the papers were full of a ghastly murder in Bournemouth, when the body of a young girl had been found in one of the Chines, most foully done to death. It had happened at around midnight, hours after I got back to Clapham.

And shortly afterwards the papers carried a photograph of the accused man. It was the man who had tried to pick me up in the restaurant. I shivered with horror. If I hadn't been a happily married wife and a dedicated actress, it could have been me. For he was bent on murder that night, and his preference was for small, slightly built females.

By the strangest of coincidences too, the girl he chose lived not far from me in Ruislip, and was not keen either on meeting him that night, but he persuaded her out for a moonlight stroll, the last one she was ever to take.

His name was Neville Heath.

I read all the evidence with macabre interest when he came to trial, and I caught my breath as I read that he had been seen going into Bobby's restaurant for tea just before five on that afternoon. There was no need for me to go forward to confirm this, for many people had witnessed it, and his visit to the restaurant wasn't in doubt. The only person I told at the time was Mary, and she shuddered at the memory of our light-hearted joking over my 'click'.

I went later to see his wax figure in Madame Tussaud's, just to confirm that imagination hadn't been playing tricks and I had read too much into this casual meeting. But I wasn't mistaken. The hair, the jacket, the trousers, and above all the eyes were unmistakable.

As I stared at the flawed handsome face, flawed because I now knew of the terrible things he had done, and for which he was justly hanged, something which had eluded me until that moment suddenly fell into place. It hadn't been instinct after all which had made me so sure he was lying when he said he worked for the BBC. It was because when I told him that I worked for the BBC he hadn't asked me my name. That was the moment he had betrayed himself as a liar. The lack of curiosity was unnatural.

Small wonder that I am aghast at the chances young people will take nowadays when they accept lifts in cars from strangers. My memories are too strong, even now, of the time when a cup of tea could have led to murder most foul – with me as the victim.

And the terrible thing was that the police were hot on his trail for another ghastly murder, but some nicety of the law had prevented his photograph from being printed in the newspapers. They were actually in Bournemouth that day, going from hotel to hotel checking on the guests. Twenty-four hours made all the difference between life and death to that poor little girl from Ruislip.

Later I was to meet an actress who lived in the next flat to the other lady he had murdered, and she couldn't bring herself to speak of the atrocities he had committed, for she had been the one to find the body.

He was a monster. But he didn't look like one. Which is why he was able to commit his crimes, of course. For if murderers looked like murderers, everyone would be suspicious and wouldn't go within miles of them.

I claim no credit for recognizing the evil in the man. With a husband at home and a career to follow, I hadn't the slightest interest in him. It wasn't prescience which protected me but the solid values by which I lived.

5

Despite all the money we spent on train fares during my year in ITMA, when I was fleeing back and forth to Glasgow like a yo-yo, the habits of my thrifty childhood were strong, and I had prudently put away a tidy balance for a rainy day, and also to meet the tax demands which would certainly be made upon me. Till now, I'd never earned enough to pay tax, but with the repeat fees added to my basic ITMA fee, I knew I'd certainly find the Tax Inspector taking an interest in me.

So, with this little nest-egg to support our decision, and because I still had a few long-standing radio engagements to fulfil in London – a few Mrs Dale's Diary bookings and some 'Just So' stories for Children's Hour – Sandy and I thought it a good idea to keep on the Clapham flat for a little while longer. It wasn't expensive, and it would be better than having to find digs each time I came south. Strangely enough, family and friends enthusiastically approved. What had seemed utter madness when I first decided to divide my time between London and Glasgow now had a touch of glamour, for they had all grown used to the idea of a little foothold in London which they could share with me when they decided to visit the capital. I've always been impressed by the fact that Glaswegians are far more inclined to visit London than Londoners to visit Glasgow. To a Scot, London is tantalizingly near and an ever-beckoning challenge, whereas the average Londoner sees the land north of the border as alien unknown territory which takes some courage to penetrate.

My landlady was strangely tolerant of my overnight guests, and they were legion during my year in ITMA, for they all wanted to see the show. Mary had come up from Bournemouth, and had slept head to feet to fit into my single bed. This was no hardship, for she was one of nine children and had always slept with her sisters, and my little eyrie high above the roof-tops of London made an intriguing change from a Glasgow tenement.

When Sandy's sister Rose and husband Tom wanted to celebrate his return from the RAF they headed straight for Clapham with my ma-in-law, to the digs I had managed to find for them in the house next door. But when they decided to stay over for an extra night, and their landlady couldn't accommodate them as she had other visitors arriving, it seemed the most natural thing in the world that they should prefer to camp on my floor than seek pastures new. We dined off odd cups and saucers and plates, shared the cutlery between us, and found the whole atmosphere so different from the douce entertaining done in Glasgow that every meal became a hilarious picnic.

Everything was excused on the grounds that 'after all, they were only digs'. I decided this was my favourite form of entertaining, for I need feel no sense of guilt at the lack of any of the finer touches, as the background was not mine.

Everyone entered into this light-hearted attitude. When Muriel, my friend from the Glasgow factory, homed straight to me like a trained pigeon when the FANY were finished with her, and brought a chum and two boy friends in tow, everybody in the house lent their treasures for the party. Lois whisked through with her best china and tea trolley, the Finches ran up with extra cutlery, Miss Chree supplied her finest teapot, Mrs Parker wheezed in with two lovely lace tray-cloths, and if the champagne was drunk not from glasses, but from cups, at least the cups were of the most delicate bone china. We had toast after toast to celebrate our first peacetime reunion, and the very shortcomings of the trappings added to the bohemian atmosphere, while the whole house seemed to ring with laughter as all shared the champagne.

Muriel and her friends were enchanted to be given tickets for ITMA, which had been their one continuing link with home while they were overseas, and if I'd arranged an introduction to the King and Queen themselves I couldn't have impressed them more than I did when I introduced them to Tommy Handley afterwards. Not all the gold in Fort Knox could have bought those tickets, and I was pleased to be able to make their first entertainment in London such an exciting occasion, for I felt we owed so much to our returning servicemen and women.

I am one of those people who keep their friends for life, but I never saw Muriel again after that night. When I see people drinking liquor out of cups in theatre dressing rooms when too many visitors turn up and glasses run out, I am instantly reminded of our champagne party in Clapham all those years ago. I wonder if Muriel too remembers, and is as amazed as I am at my temerity in giving parties in my one room in Clapham, with assorted dishes and cutlery from every corner of the house. Maybe that's why she vanished without trace!

I was particularly glad of my threequarter-size bed when another sister-in-law and her little girl came down to spend a week with me, and even more so when Ma, my mother-in-law, travelled down with me when I had a few broadcasts to do, for she was an adorable little dumpling who needed every inch of space I could spare. But we never even felt the discomfort of the head-to-toe sleeping arrangement, so pleased were we to be exploring London together. She had worked there as a girl, and had been married in St Paul's Church in Knightsbridge. One day she wondered aloud, rather wistfully, it seemed to me, what had happened to her marriage certificate, which had disappeared when it had been sent away for some wartime purpose and never returned. So I said, 'Well, let's go to St Paul's and ask for another one.' She giggled nervously at the thought of what they would say 'if an auld wife like her went in for such a document after all those years', but I assured her that nothing could frighten me after our pantomime on the Tube in getting from Euston to Clapham. And a pantomime it had been, and no mistake. I was carrying my best Breton sailor velour hat in a hat-box in one hand, a suitcase in the other, and at the same time trying to prod a reluctant ma-in-law on to the escalator. She was terrified of this moving stairway, but I told her there was nothing to it, and pushed her forward, after counting 'One, two, three – *now*!' She got one foot on the tread, but before she could pick up her other foot, which seemed paralysed with fright, down she went at my feet like a ninepin.

I couldn't let go my cases, for the escalator was packed and there wasn't a free spot to lay them down, and in any case I could never have picked Ma up, weighing as she did a good eleven stone or more. A wee RAF chap pushed through to us, tucked his cap safely under his shoulder tab, put both arms under Ma's armpits and, breathing deeply, heaved with all his strength and got her to her feet. His task was made no easier by the fact that both Ma and I were pealing with hysterical laughter. When we got safely to the bottom, this Galahad of the Air Force still holding on to her, down she went again with sheer relief, apparently, at having reached *terra firma*. We all three of us leaned against the Tube wall, gasping with laughter, in Ma's case laced with terror at the thought of having to go through it all again at the Clapham end, but this time on an upwards moving escalator.

Weak from hiccups and hysteria, we thanked our gallant RAF lad and boarded the train for Clapham. At the other end, I again counted, 'One, two, three – *NOW*!,' and this time Ma nipped on like a bird, firmly assisted by me, for I'd laid down both case and hat-box to leave my hands free and keep her upright as far as was humanly possible. We couldn't rely on somebody coming to our rescue twice! To my horror, I saw that the strap of the hat-box had caught itself between the moving stairs. Tug as I might, I couldn't free it. We were almost at the top, and I was desperate. My best hat was trapped inside. I thrust my fingers towards the top stair, and the next moment found myself seized by an inspector who had been watching, unknown to me, and who was now galvanized into activity by my folly. 'Take your fingers away *AT ONCE*,' he roared. 'Those blades will have them off – they're like scythes!' I'd had no idea those things at the top of the escalator were blades! I leaped back as if I'd been stung by a wasp. With a twist of his wrist he'd freed the strap, and we were all safely by the exit, no harm done. But I had nightmares for quite a long while afterwards when I thought of having exposed my precious typing fingers to such risk, all unwittingly. It was just like being back at school, when I'd relived for weeks the horror of the time we'd played at slides down the 'mountains' in Paddy Orr's park, heedless of our speed or danger until a chum had plummeted straight into the wall and split her head wide open. Did one never learn? I wondered. And was there danger everywhere?

Anyway, after such an experience and such a dressing down from the inspector for my stupidity, a mere request for a marriage certificate was nothing, and I assured Ma that we would travel by bus and not go near the Underground or on to escalators travelling in any direction. We found St Paul's Church without difficulty, but took an age to find anyone to speak to on such a sunny summery afternoon when everyone seemed to be in the streets or in the parks; at last a little door opened as we hovered outside, wondering whether or not to knock, and out popped a dark-robed gentleman, who took us into his office and listened to us most courteously. Ma was thrilled to the point of tears when he looked up the register and found the entry and said there would be no difficulty at all in supplying a copy. He would post it to her care of the Clapham address. She handed over the necessary cash, and we left the church, Ma starry-eyed and almost walking on air. I was so glad, in the light of later events, that I had suggested this ploy. It meant such a lot to her. When the certificate eventually arrived she gazed at the slip of paper as though with it had come all the happiness she had shared with her long-dead much-loved husband.

Without my jobs in London and my little room to return to, such adventures would have been unthinkable, and it made for a lovely sense of freedom to be able to whisk down to London at a moment's notice, without any worry over packing or accommodation, and to be able to share this background with my nearest and dearest.

When I had to leave Ma for my rehearsals, it was a lucky coincidence that Miss Chree was 'resting' at the time (as a freelance housekeeper she was often out of work), and was able to keep her company. Both of them Aberdonians, they got on like a house on fire, and I think it was one of the rare occasions when my dear Miss Chree was able to relax with a kindred spirit, with no need to be on her guard, or translate her spontaneous flow of speech into 'English' for ears unfamiliar with the Scottish tongue. It was also one of the rare occasions when she could be homely and chatty, like a suburban housewife with time on her hands, and exchange family background tales with someone who knew every inch of the territory she was describing, the school she had attended, and the distillery where she had worked as a girl. It was a very happy time for both of them, for Ma also knew and understood the London scene, where she had worked as a girl, and when I'd return from rehearsals or recordings I'd find them both laughing over some remembered youthful indiscretion, cheeks flushed, soft voices in harmony, enjoying a cup of tea and some Romary's special wheaten biscuits, a quality biscuit much appreciated by both, and which they had learned to enjoy in the kitchens of the rich houses where they had given loving and unstinting service. Ma had worked in the nursery, and the great ones had valued her soft tones and gentle authority, and from them she had learned never to raise her voice in anger. 'If you shout at the children, they will shout back at you,' she had been instructed. So she had the quiet tones of a lady, and Sandy and his brother Jimmy also had the quietest voices in Springburn, I believe. Miss Chree, as a free-lance, didn't have the same perks as Ma in the matter of holidays in Scotland for the grouse season, or on the south coast with the children while their parents were abroad, but she had her tales and titbits too, to keep up her end of the story-swopping. Of her housekeeping for Richard Addinsell, when he was collaborating and writing for Joyce Grenfell, and of how Joyce Grenfell had come back after their very first broadcast together, when they'd both been petrified, and had flopped into a chair and declared, 'I'll *never* get into such a state of nerves again. It simply isn't worth it, and it all went *beautifully*.' As, of course, it did. I wondered if she'd been able to keep to that resolve? If she had, I envied her from the bottom of my heart, for I was always plagued with fluttering 'butterflies' whatever I did.

Miss Chree deliberately adopted a fierce demeanour for her scatty employers, whom she considered required keeping in order, and she made me whoop with laughter when she told Ma and me of the occasion when she'd scolded Addinsell for putting crumbs into the sink with the dishes, which he'd left for her to do in the morning. Naturally, the crumbs swelled and choked the sink, and she found a disgusting mess of cigarette ends and food debris which sent her charging into his bedroom to announce in tones of thunder, '*Never* put crumbs down that sink again, or I walk out of this house and never come back.' The next week, after a party, following a successful show for which he'd written the music and to which all the top names in show business had been invited, he made even Miss Chree smile with his description of the drama of the table-clearing when he'd rushed round his famous guests, and implored them, 'Don't put a single crumb into the sink, or Miss Chree will shake the dust of this flat off the soles of her feet for ever.' She threw back her head and laughed with me, and with Ma. 'Can you imagine it,' she said, 'Diana Wynyard and Diana Churchill and all those grand folk scraping their plates on to sheets of newspaper, just because I showed Addinsell how it ought to be done!' She really adored him, and found he had a great sense of humour, and was sorry when that post had to be given up because he was going abroad for some time and giving up the flat.

She was equally forthright when she found that the French top-ranking officer, with the dark dramatic swirling cloak, and handsome face, was sharing his flat and his bed with an ordinary sailor! She was more worldly-wise than I, for I would never have appreciated the significance of such a thing, coming as I did from crowded tenements where everybody shared beds as a matter of course. But Miss Chree had lived in London for years and knew the wickedness of their ways in the capital. With tremendous courage, finding the AB's cap and coat hanging in the hall when she arrived in the morning, she had marched into the bedroom, and uttered the ultimatum, 'Out of that bed – or I walk out of the front door.' I gasped at her daring. I could never have done it. I couldn't have found the words. I wouldn't, of course, have known that it was necessary to utter such sentiments. She won that battle hands down, and all the rest of the time that officer remained in London she never saw anything out of place.

Of the Egyptian Ambassador she spoke very highly, and it was a revelation to hear her imitate his slow strange accent. Apparently he had been robbed of quite a few *objets d'art*, and suspected a casual worker in the house, so he laid a trap for him and caught him. 'He became over-confident,' he said to Miss Chree, slowly and carefully finding the English words for his philosophy. 'You see, the thief stupidly imagines that the person from whom he is stealing is so foolish that he does not miss the leetle things which are being taken. So if something is left in an obvious place, he takes it, and so is trapped. How is it possible he can believe the possessor can be so unaware of hees possessions?' I was most impressed with this reasoning, and even more intrigued that this Middle East diplomat should express his conclusions to Miss Chree, confident that his wisdom was being distilled in a quarter where it would be appreciated.

One of her distinguished employers informed her, on arrival, that his wife was in a nursing home, but would be returning within a week or ten days. There were two charming children, cared for by a nannie, and cupboards and drawers filled with the most exquisite clothing and underclothes that Miss Chree had ever seen. Sheer silks, with priceless embroidery, furs, velvets and brocades; house-coats, nighties and undies worth a king's ransom. Miss Chree imagined some beautiful creature of a delicate grace to wear such finery, and could hardly wait to cast her eyes on the lady of the house. On the day of her return, Miss Chree was in the kitchen preparing a meal to suit the family celebration. She was longing to peep into the hall when she heard voices, but she couldn't leave her pastry or her oven. After ten minutes or so, she heard the sound of high-pitched laughter, the kitchen door was flung open, and she found herself staring at a wild-eyed woman who was stark naked! 'Mad!' she said to me. 'Quite mad. Her hair a mass of tangles, and eyes shining like a tiger about to spring.' 'What did you do, Miss Chree,' I asked, wondering how on earth I'd have met the same situation. 'I just picked up the pepper pot,' she said unexpectedly, 'and I told her if she took another step I'd throw it in her eyes.' She sighed sadly, 'All those beautiful clothes for her homecoming. All that pretence about a nursing home when she must have been in a lunatic asylum. And all those hopes for a cure dashed within ten minutes of her coming into the house. And those lovely children, with that blood in them.'

I was full of admiration, though, for her thinking of the pepper pot so quickly, for that had been my own chosen ammunition against the day when a German paratrooper might land in our garden in Glasgow, but I, after all, had had years to think of such a thing and Miss Chree had been taken completely by surprise. She was clearly a resourceful character, and I was right to trust her judgement so implicitly. It was a great comfort to know she lived in the same house, and that when I was returning for work I was also returning to her.

I think Ma would have been quite pleased to stay on for

a bit longer in London, but not only were my broadcasts finished, I had Sandy and the McFlannels waiting for me.

At that time in Scotland the McFlannels' radio show was the same compulsive listening on a Saturday night as ITMA was on Thursdays all over the country, and as far as the Scots were concerned there was no doubt which of my characters they preferred. Tattie McIntosh might be known throughout the world, thanks to ITMA's fame, but in Scotland she wasn't a patch on the gallus Ivy McTweed. Helen Pryde had written this part for me, and told me that when she wrote Ivy's dialogue she could hear my voice in every word. Indeed, in one of her books, now a treasured possession, she wrote: 'Ivy McTweed is you, and no other voice than yours will ever be able to interpret her dialogue and irrepressible cheerfulness so faithfully.'

Now that ITMA was finished and I could spend much more time in Glasgow, Ivy became a regular member of the cast, instead of just being written in when I was sure to be north of the border, and it was the greatest fun working with Meg Buchanan (Sarah McFlannel), John Morton (Willie), Willie Joss (Uncle Mattha), Grace McChlery (Mrs Mc-Cotton), Elsie Payne (wee Ian), and, of course, my boy friend Peter and his sister Maisie, and a host of other characters who came in from time to time, including Rikki Fulton. Rikki was a bit of an amateur fortune-teller at that time, although I doubt if even he could have predicted just what a big star he himself was to become, able to pack the Pavilion to the roof with his comic characterizations and his great duo with Jack Milroy as 'Francie and Josie'. Unable to resist the lure of having my palm read, with cards thrown in as a bonus, I was sent into shivers of delight when Rikki solemnly assured me that I was destined for fame and fortune in the theatre in London, and that I must on no account think of giving up my career. I wanted to believe him, and yet what were we to do with our private lives, Sandy and I? His job was in Glasgow, our real house was there, and would it really be possible to live between Clapham and Glasgow for an indefinite period? My mind was in a whirl of mixed emotions. Ambition was strong. I'd had a dangerous taste of real fame in ITMA, and although I knew now I could get plenty of work in Glasgow, London was still the place which held West End Theatre, television, films and great radio shows of nation-wide popularity. Sandy's suggestion of going to London 'to get the acting bug out of my system' didn't seem to be working too well! He told me now not to worry, just to take things as they came, and meantime he was happily getting his handicap down on the golf course while I was chasing the bright lights! We always had a perfect understanding, and he knew it was a divine discontent which drove me south, not any desire to get away from him.

There was one other who was convinced my future lay in London and that was my dear friend Joan Harben, the beloved Mona Lott of ITMA. When I went down again to fulfil some broadcasting engagements, Joan and I had lunch together and she thought it would be an excellent idea if I were to apply for membership of the Repertory Players. This company was composed of professional actors, actresses and directors who were prepared to put on a Sunday-night performance of any new play, without salary, rehearsed and produced just as though it were destined for a long run, and to which all the top managements were invited to consider its possibilities as a West End success. Many plays were dead on paper, or managements were blind to their virtues, but a sort of live audition with London's top actors gave them the chance to assess commercial hopes more accurately. There was great care taken with the casting, for not only was it a shop window for the actors and the playwright, but if a play transferred to the West End, the Repertory Players collected royalties as long as the play ran. This was their financial reward for all their hard work, and for their skill in recognizing a good runner on paper. Other actors attended the Sunday-night performances, for the plays when bought were often re-cast, and the actors were looking out for parts which they could chase if the play were a success.

It provided a golden opportunity, too, for the clown to play Hamlet and vice versa, and actors could play roles which no commercial management would dream of offering. The in-built heart-break, of course, was in helping to sell a Sunday-night play, and then to find your part re-cast for the West End. But it was a chance everybody was prepared to take, just to be *seen* by all the managements at once. Actors are ever optimistic, and hug the thought, 'Well if not this play, then they'll remember me for another, later.'

It wasn't easy to get into the Repertory Players, for all the obvious reasons I've given, and I was lucky to have Joan's backing, and to be accepted. They weren't optimistic of having anything for a Scottish actress, but I paid my subscription and became a member, and privately considered it was just a glorified version of the Pantheon Club and couldn't see what all the fuss was about letting me in. I didn't expect to hear a word of encouragement from them, but by one of those lucky twists of fate and timing which every actor needs, among the plays given to the committee to consider for the coming season was one by John Dighton entitled *The Happiest Days of your Life* and in that play was the part of a schoolgirl, Barbara Marshbanks, not spelt Marjoribanks. The only established actress small enough to impersonate a schoolgirl was on tour with a play which was definitely coming into the West End, and she couldn't be prised out of it. The committee rooted around for somebody who was experienced in comedy, but looked convincingly juvenile, and were unable to find her amongst their own ranks. Joan's mother, Mary Jerrold, was in a play in the West End with A. E. Matthews, with whom I'd toured in *A Play for Ronnie*, the adventures of which I've told elsewhere,[1] and she consulted Matty, as we all called him, as to my skill as an actress. Joan told me later that Matty had said, 'Well, I've just toured with that little Scots gel. She looks about twelve. We couldn't understand a damn word she was saying, but the audiences fell about, and she stole all the notices!' With such a reference from the great Matty, I was invited to read the part, and a solemn-faced committee burst into spontaneous laughter with my first line. The part was mine!

There were several splendid names connected with the production: Nigel Stock, Campbell Singer, Laurence Naismith, and Barbara Leake. And when Nigel couldn't rehearse, his part was taken by Leslie Phillips. I was astounded at anybody learning a part just to stand in for someone else for a rehearsal, especially when nobody was being paid. I didn't realize that London actors seized every opportunity to act with their peers, to keep technique shining bright, and who knew but that someone wouldn't fall out of the production and they'd play the part after all. The other actors were so busy with radio and film work that we scarcely ever had a full rehearsal with the entire company. I was at every rehearsal, though, for I had only the engagement to which I was committed and that was the tenth birthday party of the McFlannels in Glasgow, which was to take place on a Saturday two weeks before the Repertory Players' performance of *The Happiest Days of your Life*. The committee hesitated to ask any of us to turn down work, for they were well aware we worked for nothing on

[1] *A Toe on the Ladder*

the Sunday play. However, as ill-luck would have it, they became so worried at the lack of full rehearsals when the performance date was drawing ominously close that they decided nobody would be allowed to miss a single rehearsal for any reason whatsoever, otherwise the part would be re-cast.

It seemed terribly unfair to have to cancel my McFlannels' broadcast when I'd attended every single rehearsal of the unpaid play and they were truly sorry, but the decision had been made and must apply to all of us without exception.

Frantic phone calls to Helen Pryde alerted her to alter her script, for I'd promised I'd be there and she'd written me into the show. She took it very well, and I sent a telegram which was inserted into the programme, so I did take part in the celebrations in a kind of a way. But oh how I would have loved to have been there with them.

Joan Harben had heard all about my disappointment over the McFlannels from the other committee members and she told me not to be too upset. She was sure the sacrifice would be worth it, for the whisper had gone round that we were on to a winner which was destined for the West End, and unless the management which bought it were stark staring mad, I'd go with it. With the author's permission I had actually been allowed to change the name of the character I was playing. It was really Sandy who gave me the courage to suggest this. The word-play on the names 'Marshbanks not spelt Marjoribanks' had struck us both as being very English, but I'd never have dreamed of saying so had he not encouraged me to think up a Scottish equivalent to match my accent and nationality. We both sat with wrinkled brows, trying out all possible permutations of Scottish names, when suddenly I remembered a pair of school chums, one of whose names was spelt Cahoun, and the other Colquhoun.

Experimentally I tried out my idea. 'Barbara Cahoun, *not* spelt Colk-a-hown.' Even to our ears it sounded much funnier than the Marjoribanks joke. When I tried it out on the English ears of the author, he was delighted.

'*Far* better,' he said generously, '*far* funnier – we'll use it.' I knew his was the final word, for the committee had had to seek his permission in the first place as to whether or not he had any objections to the part being played in Scots when it had in fact been written for an English schoolgirl. And again he had been kind and encouraging in saying that the lines gained a funnier dimension delivered in my Scottish lilt.

When the programmes were printed and I gazed at the names, 'Barbara Cahoun . . . Molly Weir', I felt a stab of real pleasure from this tiny contribution of my very own my very first christening of a fictional character.

It was prophetic that I had named her and that I created her, for when the curtain went down on that fateful Sunday night a packed house rose and applauded us to the echo, and every management in London was bidding for the right to put *The Happiest Days of your Life* on in the West End. Tennents won. And, apart from one of their contract players, I was the only member of the Repertory Players who was cast for the West End production. It seemed a great shame, after all the hard work put in by the rest of the company, but they were philosophical, and it didn't do them any harm, judging from their later successes.

But I was stunned by the immediate proof that managements are no good at reading plays 'cold', for every single one of them had had that play to read and every single one of them had turned it down. John Dighton was well known as a writer for films and nobody took him seriously as a playwright, so dismissed his play as no good. But one Repertory Players' production of it showed managements their mistake, and the rest is theatre history. It ran for two years in the West End, was performed by every repertory company in the country, was translated for abroad, and became a successful film. But all that was to come.

Meantime, before I left for home, I had been invited to a special performance of ITMA at which all the Royal Family were to be present. I was agog with excitement. I would never have such a good chance of being so close to Royalty, for the Paris is a very small theatre, and I would even be presented as an ex-member of the show.

The night before the performance the telephone rang. It was Sandy, from Glasgow. We rang one another all the time, so I sensed no danger. In the midst of my bubbling excitement over the Royal ITMA, he said quietly, 'Ma has been taken very ill. Will you come home?' My heart turned over. I adored Sandy's mother, but we had been together so recently, I couldn't believe it was serious. Indeed, I had tried to coax her to come down with me on this occasion, but she had refused because she was going to her brother's golden wedding a few weeks later, and felt she must stop so much gadding about. 'What train will I get?' I asked. 'The show finishes tomorrow about nine-thirty, and I can either get the . . . ' but Sandy broke in, 'Come tomorrow on the 1.30 p.m. and I'll meet you and take you straight to Springburn.' I didn't make a single protest. If Sandy felt it was all that urgent, then it was. 'I'll get the one-thirty,' I said.

I went in to Miss Chree in a daze. I started to tell her what Sandy had said and I burst into tears. 'It must be very serious,' I sobbed, 'for Sandy knows about the Royal ITMA and still he wants me to come home immediately.' Miss Chree was very distressed, for she felt she too was hearing of a dear friend's suffering, now that she had met Ma and shared her memories with her.

'Come on now, lassie,' she said, 'we'll ha'e a wee cup o' tea, and then we'll just put a few things into a case. You'll need your sleep, and I'll help you to do what's necessary in the morning.'

I rang Kavanagh's office next day and told them I wouldn't require my precious ticket after all, and I caught the one-thirty for Glasgow. Sandy's face was tense and worn. Ma was in a coma. For five days we tended her, and took it in turns to sit up all night with her. I so admired Sandy when it was his time to watch by the bedside. I'd hear him in the night saying gently to her, 'Ma. Ma. It's Sandy. Can you hear me?' But she made no response. I was terrified to say such words when I took his place, for I feared she might open her eyes and there would be no recognition in them, and I wouldn't be able to bear it.

A district nurse came and helped us to turn Ma over in bed, and held whispered consultations as we bathed Ma's face and combed her thick heavy hair. I don't know why we whispered, for dear Ma heard nothing, but it seemed wrong somehow to speak in our ordinary voices.

After five days the nurse decided it was too much for all of us, and so they removed Ma to Stobhill Hospital and Sandy went with her in the ambulance, but after a few hours they sent him home, promising to send for him the moment there was any change. It might go on for days, and there was no point in his staying. But she slipped away before he had reached the house, where all of us waited, and our next telephone call told us it was all over.

It was a nightmare. I wanted to wake up and find everything just as it had been. I couldn't face the knowledge that all that gentle wisdom had gone from us. But she hadn't suffered. We clung to that, as we clung to one another for comfort. She had just stumbled a little on her way to bed, fallen asleep, gone into a coma and never wakened. It is a gentle ending many crave, but I feel our leave-taking of life should have much more positive awareness. We should *know* what is happening. I passionately agree with Dylan Thomas, 'Do not go gentle into that good night. Rage, rage, against the dying of the light.'

And it was then that I remembered her desire for the marriage certificate. Perhaps that was another sign that we hadn't recognized at the time. There was a small grain of comfort that I, with my little room in Clapham, had made it easy for her to collect this precious document, which had meant so much to her. And then another thought struck me. If she had come with me to London, as I had wanted, she would have died in my little room, and how would we have got her home again? Maybe some deep instinct, unrecognized, had warned her not to leave Glasgow, although no outward sign betrayed anything was amiss.

It was a time of infinite sadness, and I couldn't arouse any enthusiasm for rehearsals for this play which was to change so much in our lives afterwards.

6

Ma's death affected me almost as badly as Grannie's had done all those years ago. I couldn't shake off a terrible lethargy, and I would waken in the morning with the tears running down my cheeks. Sandy too was badly affected, and we did what we could to find solace in the fact that she had had a peaceful end. I was only roused out of my dream-like state by a letter from Lois, my friendly Post Office lass in the next room at Clapham, and I let out such a piercing shriek that Sandy thought I'd cut myself to the bone with a knife, for I was in the kitchen at the time. He was furious with me for the fright I'd given him, and it was the first real fierce emotion we'd expressed since Ma's death. It seemed strange to feel the adrenalin flowing again, and almost to enjoy an argument.

Lois's letter confirmed something which I had always feared might happen, and I was furious. She was a very gentle, softly spoken girl, and had been converted to the Catholic faith some time before I went to Clapham. Like all converts, she was more conscientious in her belief than a natural-born Catholic and she filled her spare time with various prayers and observances, and seemed overwhelmed with the business of daily living. I think all the wartime coupons and ration books got her down, and she was despondent that she was still using them so long after the war had finished. Saturdays were devoted to cleaning and sweeping out her little room and I used to laugh at her despair over this task, I who had a whole house to flee round each time I went back to Glasgow, *plus* my Clapham room. I used to say to her half-joking, wholly warningly, 'Now don't you think of going into a convent.' I felt the peaceful life there had a terrific attraction, although she never mentioned such a thing, and I was afraid she was becoming less and less able to cope with the stresses and strains of ordinary life. She just laughed at me, as we sipped our tea, and ate our hoarded chocolates and I comforted myself with the thought that she'd never be able to give up her endless cups of tea, so my fears were probably groundless.

Now the letter told me that my sixth sense had been right. She couldn't bear to tell me face to face, but wrote to say that she had left her job and when I returned to London she would be resident in the big Catholic church along the road, preparatory to going to France to study for her future life as a nun.

I could hardly wait to get down there to rescue her from what I saw as oblivion. Miss Chree shared my views. 'Unpaid domestics,' she said, 'that delicate girl. It's a shame, but there's nothing you can do about it. They get carried away with the idea, and the church encourages it, for they get free domestics who work till they drop.'

But there was something I could at least try to do about it. I marched along to the church and I saw the Mother Superior. I begged to be allowed to see Lois, and I was frank and said that I hoped to talk her out of this decision to bury herself in a convent. The Mother Superior was gentle, and her eyes twinkled, but she was firm in her refusal to let me meet Lois, who could not be disturbed. I was shattered. I told her that we were frightened of nuns when we were children. That their clothes were an anachronism in modern times, and that it was surely a shame to shut themselves away from the world when Christ himself said, 'Go ye into all the world and preach the gospel.' That the true virtue was to live in the world and influence people by the shining example of beautiful behaviour. The cheek of me! She just shook her head smilingly and said that the world needed the prayers of the faithful, and that their particular prayers had a concentration which could surely help all mankind. I could see Lois when she returned from France, and before she was placed in whatever order had been decided upon, but I could not see her now. And that was that.

Lois went to Angers in France for her 'instruction', and she wrote to me from there and said that when she worked with the little nursery-school-age children and saw all their little smocks and rows of tiny shoes she was reminded of me and of my passion for footwear and summery clothes. She sounded so normal and so like herself that I was faintly reassured, and when I saw her, only once, after she returned, I was so glad they hadn't shaved off her lovely auburn hair. Apparently this rule was altered after the terrible head-shaving meted out to collaborationists in France during the war, and I patted her top-knot of silky hair under her head-dress to make sure it was all there in all its glory. She looked peaceful and content, and said it was wonderful to own nothing of her own but a cross and a breviary. She had let me pay something towards these possessions as my farewell present, and she had given me the tea-trolley once gladly lent for the champagne party for Muriel, and the rolled gold bracelet which had been her twenty-first birthday present. I have both to this day.

We still write to one another, and she has read my other books, but when I remember her relief at owning only two things, and sharing all else with her other Sisters of Mercy, I feel sure in my heart that it was the complication of wartime Britain with its red tape, its coupons, and points, and rationed food which drove her to seek peace within the walls of a convent. She is in a teaching order now, and seems happy, and however hard I tried to argue her out of this enclosed life at the time, I feel greatly privileged to know I have a special place in her prayers.

No wonder I didn't want Lois to find me fully clothed in bed in the morning after that Savoy party when I imbibed not wisely but too well! Fancy being found in such a condition by a future nun! Dear Lois, I couldn't have inflicted that on her for all the tea in China. I wonder if she found it difficult to overcome her thirst for tea, and for sweet things? Sometimes the small sacrifices are harder than the larger abstinences.

But if Lois had separated herself from me, her departure brought my dear Miss Chree closer, for I urged her to ask Mrs Parker if she could have Lois's room and so share the top floor with me. It was an extra flight of stairs, true, but it was large and sunny, and needed far fewer shillings to heat it than the narrow darker room downstairs. And she would get it at the same rent if she moved fast, before it could be advertised to a stranger at a higher figure. I felt, rightly, that the landlady couldn't possibly ask Miss Chree for more money when I knew to a penny what Lois had been paying. And so it proved. Jubilant, we trotted up and down those stairs a hundred times carrying books, and wee stools, and an assortment of treasures, but by nightfall she was installed, and the neat austerity of Lois's room had been transformed to the rakish, book-strewn clutter which was Miss Chree's preferred environment.

I told her she must give the employment agency my telephone number, and she could now ring in regularly instead of having to spend fares going all the way into

London. I had given Mr Finch downstairs this freedom too – he was in show business, on the stage management side, and I knew only too well the inconvenience of being without a telephone to deny this facility to anyone who needed it. It made no difference to me, as the room was never locked, for they, my neighbours, were all sea-green incorruptibly honest, and it was good to know that when the telephone rang somebody would answer it, and no jobs would be missed for any of us. Miss Chree set herself the task of ensuring that everybody who used the telephone would leave the coins on the wee saucer in payment for the calls!

I had signed my contract with H. M. Tennent, the same management for whom I had done *A Play for Ronnie*, and the moment had arrived for us to go into rehearsal for *The Happiest Days of your Life*. The director of *A Play for Ronnie* would also direct *The Happiest Days*, so there would be no feeling of strangeness with him, thank goodness. Only Betty Wolfe, the contract player, and I were from the Repertory Players' production, and all the others would be new to us. I was consumed with curiosity to find out who they were, and thrilled beyond measure to discover that the part of the headmistress was to be played by marvellous Margaret Rutherford. Like almost everyone else in London, I had adored her in *Blithe Spirit* and had seen her in many shows, and I fairly shook with excitement at the mere thought of working on the same stage with her. Her husband, Stringer, was also in the play, taking the part of one of the parents, for the play was concerned with a boys' and girls' school having to share the same premises, and keeping the knowledge from all the parents.

We assembled on the stage of the Haymarket Theatre for the read-through of the play, after a brief introduction to one another, and it felt very strange to me to be reading from the script again, having given a public performance all those weeks ago. It was also most interesting to judge the variation in reading and style compared with the Repertory Players' company.

George Howe as the headmaster had a lovely fussiness which I liked, and Colin Gordon a caustic quality which was later to win him the award as the best supporting actor of that year. The wee lad who was playing Hopcroft, my fellow-conspirator in the school ploys, had most odd-coloured hair I thought, and was astounded to learn that it was dyed! And him only fifteen! However, it was all in the cause of art, for he was playing one of the ginger-headed children in *Life with Father* and was quite fed-up at having to go to have this messy hair-dyeing done every fortnight because his hair grew so fast that the roots showed!

Margaret Rutherford was quite entrancing to watch. So gentle, and so quiet in herself, but all fierceness and twitching and affronted outrage when she became the headmistress. There were those who hinted that Margaret didn't know what she was doing, and that she was simply being herself, so that all comedy effects were quite accidentally achieved. I, watching her at rehearsal, knew better. I saw her work out a brilliant and tricky piece of sleight-of-hand with a large knife which had to be swept out of sight, before presenting a smiling innocent face to her arch-enemy, the headmaster. And I, with the others, was convulsed with laughter as she improvised with the telephone cord until she was completely entangled. And yet I was also puzzled by the gentle air of pathos which clung to her like a perfume when she was in repose. As I grew to know her better, and to love her, I gradually reached the conclusion that the tragedy of Margaret was that she possessed the soul of a sweet, light, fairy-like creature which had somehow strayed and been trapped in that large grotesque body. And when she looked in the mirror, the beauty of feature which she expected couldn't be reconciled with that pursing mouth and those quivering chins. I felt she longed to be soft and serious, but she was always asked to be the buffoon, and the affront somehow showed in her eyes. Her complete innocence and her vulnerability made one long to protect her, and I was so glad that in Stringer Davis she had found the perfect partner. They had a mutual love of poetry, and Stringer also delighted her with his musical gifts, for he was a talented composer of rippling little piano pieces. He used to take the actual notes of the birds, and continue them to make tunes, and sometimes even put words to them. I was entranced to hear him sing one day, to the notes of the song of the robin:

> 'I'm a little robin who loves humans,
> I'd have been a gardener if I could,
> With a glade of my own
> And a spade of my own.
> I'm a little robin who LOVES humans'.

Always, during the years of our future friendship, I chose a card with a robin for Stringer at Christmas, and added the words, 'I'm a little robin who loves humans', and his eyes would twinkle with pleasure that I had remembered his little tribute to the robin who followed him round the garden, perching on the spade, and showing proper gratitude for all the hard work involved in turning up enough worms to stock the larder.

He was a great strength to Margaret, and although hers was assuredly the greater talent, it was soon evident to managements and film moguls that if they wished to include Margaret in their cast, then they must also find a part for Stringer. This they gladly did, for Stringer was a competent actor, and, as he laughingly told me many years later, 'I'm actually beginning to learn how to be a film actor, Molly. It's just practice, of course, but I'm really getting the hang of it, after thirty years, and I get little notices all my own for my small character appearances.' He had no vanity in this respect, and simply enjoyed working with his beloved wife, and taking care of the transport, and the food, and removing all domestic worries from her brilliant shoulders. She needed no protection from rudeness or vulgarity, for her own ladylike qualities and childlike purity impressed everyone who worked with her, from stage-doorkeeper to supporting players, and I never knew the roughest stage-hand who would have said even so mild an expletive as 'damn' in her presence. If one such word did slip out under strain, there was an instant apology, although Margaret had betrayed not the slightest sign that she had heard. But this was her effect upon people. We were all a little better than our best in her presence.

I was very intrigued to find out that leading ladies engaged their own dressers, whom they kept with them for years. Margaret's was a great character, a small, slim, fair little woman with a deceptively quiet serious manner. Her name was Blanche, and I was to come to know her very well during the eight weeks of the tour of the play, when she and I shared digs. Her husband was also a dresser, and was never out of work, for he dressed Ivor Novello, whom Blanche called 'Mr Ivor'. Indeed, I was astounded to discover that when husband Bill was indisposed, Blanche went along herself and undertook the dressing of Mr Ivor! 'Blanche,' I exclaimed, horrified, 'surely men actors don't have lady dressers! You don't help him on and off with his trousers, do you?'

She was quite unmoved. 'Course I do, you daft ha'porth,' she said. 'Mr Ivor is far too busy to pay any attention to me, and I'm far too busy with all those uniforms to pay any attention to anything else but the clothes.' I had to believe her, although I was surprised at her husband Bill acquiescing to such goings-on! I couldn't see Sandy allowing me to swop places with him under similar circumstances.

Sandy and I knew we wouldn't be able to see one another until the play opened in London, for the tour was going to eight number one dates, but only in England and Wales, and as I'd be travelling every Sunday to my next theatre, there would be no free time. But at least there was no doubt that with this play we *would* open in London, and he would be out front to watch me make my London début in the West End. My stomach did somersaults at the mere thought, but it was too far away to worry about it unnecessarily. The tour had to come first.

It was a bitter winter, and the spring of 1948 was a long time a-coming. We opened in Brighton, which wasn't too far away, so the train journey, although cold, was short, but my nervous traumas over the first-night ordeal weren't helped by the fact that the digs into which I'd booked had two cats. I've always had a phobia about such creatures, and this pair had cat flu, and moped, and coughed and sneezed all over the house, and their owner was so devoted to them that I had to hide my terror and try to pretend a sympathy which was far from genuine. As I stood waiting to open the study door on that opening night, what with the thought of the first-night audience, and the knowledge that I'd have to go back to a house with two ailing cats, my hand shook so much and my teeth rattled so nervously that Duggie Ives, who played the porter, looked at me keenly to see if I were going to faint. 'I've never seen anybody so nervous in all my life,' he said. 'Buck up, they can't eat you!'

I closed my eyes, praying for courage as I waited for my cue. I heard Colin Gordon say the line, I wrenched the door open, and I catapulted on to the stage. There was a roar of laughter, as I swept all the sports impedimenta off the table, where they were neatly fielded by Colin, and we were away on a wave of warm applause. I had a round of applause on my exit, and I raced upstairs to the dressing room, eyes shining, cats forgotten.

We took curtain after curtain at the end, and we knew *The Happiest Days of your Life* had fulfilled the promise of the Sunday-night Repertory Players' performance. We were assuredly a success. At the party in the bar afterwards the brothers De Marney were among the guests, and were furious to discover I wasn't really a schoolgirl. I couldn't see that it mattered. I must have *looked* and *behaved* convincingly enough if they really had thought I was no more than thirteen. But they had apparently wanted to be in the presence of a child genius, and felt defrauded! Binkie Beaumont, Tennents' god-like presiding genius, had been right about my pigtails, though. I had at-first bunched my hair on either side of my head, and tied them in ribbons, under the impression that pigtails were a much too obvious attempt to look juvenile. After the dress rehearsal that day he had said crisply, 'Pigtails, please, for Miss Weir.' Not only had I been surprised at his noticing such a detail, I was astounded that his decision was final. There was no argument. Pigtails he had asked for, and pigtails he must get. So Betty Wolfe had criss-crossed my hair, which I then wore in a page-boy style, into two little pigtails which stuck out like Topsy's, and tied each with a navy-blue ribbon. And I had to admit the effect was funny, and realistic. As somebody said, I looked exactly like one of those terrible schoolgirls of Giles, or a refugee from St Trinian's. Those first pigtails only boasted two little criss-crosses, but by the end of the London run, Betty and I used to measure the fast growth of my hair by the extra 'cross' which was added, as month followed month. At the end of the run I had twelve crossed braids, and my hair was half-way to my waist. But all that was to come.

We played to packed houses before moving north to Newcastle, where Blanche and I shared our first digs, and not only did I have no cats to contend with, I had her hilarious company. The house was absolutely perishing, and Blanche would cast her eyes fearfully upwards towards the bedrooms as we ate our supper and chatted with our landlady, dreading the moment when we'd have to move to our Siberian quarters. I nearly choked with laughter as I chewed, for Blanche was adept at responding to the land-lady's conversation with dead-pan face, while at the same time grimacing towards the ceiling the moment the land-lady's attention was diverted to move a dish or two. Blanche literally wore more to bed than she did during the day. She used to call me through to inspect her when she was in bed, and I used to laugh myself silly at the spectacle she presented. Under thick wincyette pyjamas she wore husband Bill's long combinations, bedsocks, and his winter vest. On top went a thick cardigan, and on her head a woollen hat. I'd *never* seen anyone, not even my grannie, wear a hat to bed, and the whole appearance added up to something from a music-hall sketch. I was the perfect audience for such dressing up, and our laughter helped us to forget the icy conditions for a few minutes each night.

I enraged the dresser, though, in my efforts to keep warm. The rest of us shared a dresser between us, and it was her duty to wash and press our clothes and hang them ready for us, and to assist anyone who required such help to dress if there were quick changes. During this bitter weather it was agony to have to exchange my heavy woollen jersey, in which I'd arrived at the theatre, for the thin white poplin school blouse I wore as Barbara. One night, as my teeth chattered in a very cold dressing room, I realized I was wearing a thin navy-blue cashmere sweater, a treasured purchase of my mother at the Barrows, for none of us could afford cashmere new from the shops in those days, and of such a fine quality that my blouse would easily go on top. The dresser never helped me with my dressing, for I had always plenty of time, and so she was unaware of my scheme. Later that week, she came into the dressing room and said thoughtfully, 'I've been watching the play from the gallery, and I can't understand why that blouse of yours looks so grubby, Molly. It's washed twice a week, and as I have two anyway they never really get dirty.'

I pressed my lips together, tried to look innocent, and remained silent. This was so unusual that she looked me straight in the eye, then let her breath out in a long gasp. She seized me by the arm. 'Have you been wearing something underneath it?' she demanded, more outraged than if I'd confessed I'd gone on stage without my blue school bloomers. I nodded, thinking she was making a great fuss about nothing. She rolled up my cuff and recoiled. '*navy-blue*,' she hissed, '*navy-blue*.' She was undoing the buttons at a great speed. 'No *wonder* your blouse looked dirty. Do you realize it is *my* responsibility to keep you looking fresh and clean, and that the blame will be *mine* if the management complains.' I hadn't thought of it that way, I had to confess. I'd have owned up if they'd asked me. She whipped the comforting cashmere over my head and hung it over a chair, threw the blouse in a corner to be washed, and put on an ice-cold fresh one, ready for my next entrance. I was a great trial to her. She had already made a hole in the pocket of my gym slip because of my unforeseen habit of picking up any nails lying around the stage 'for luck' and putting them into my pocket, and she had plonked a red-hot iron and a steaming cloth over the bulge before she realized she was pressing sharp nails! I didn't hear the end of that for weeks. Schoolboys might be forgiven for such a nasty habit, she groaned, but whoever would have suspected a schoolgirl – no, she corrected herself – a grown woman indulging in such a stupid prank.

But if I was a trial to her, the understudies were to prove to be a greater one to me, after the tour was over. During the tour they had enough to occupy their minds to prevent boredom overtaking them, and we used to explore all the cities with great enthusiasm, searching out the little antique shops for bargains, and there I'd leave them to go on my own for long walks through great parks or along wintry deserted beaches, and discover the real shape of resorts when they were emptied of tourists. Maria, my Russian understudy, was plagued by an irritatingly spotty back and was thrilled when I told her that fresh yeast was considered a splendid home cure. At that she was up and away, yanking me from my book, and we presented ourselves at the side door of a big brewery and enquired politely for tuppence worth of fresh yeast. I'd had the foresight to equip myself with an empty jam-jar begged from our landlady, for we were sharing the same digs that week, and it was a nightly performance after the show, me spreading the pimply back with a layer of yeast which smelt to high heaven, and Maria spooning it from the jar and swallowing it. She reckoned a combined attack from both inside and outside must be more effective than a single solution, although what the landlady must have thought when she found her sheets reeking with stale beer fumes is anybody's guess. Maria didn't care, for the magic was working, and she was determined to parade a beautiful back to an admiring public by wearing a backless evening dress for her very first social engagement when we returned to London.

I was very surprised to find that every stage was different

in those towns we visited. Sometimes they were so shallow that our 'set' filled the space from footlights to back wall, and we had to go underneath the stage to make entrances from the other side. Occasionally they were in a deep basement, which presented other entrance problems, and it was my custom when we arrived in a strange town to go to the theatre first thing on Monday morning, lay out my make-up, etc., on my dressing-room bench, check the mail, and check exact position and entrances on the stage. In Nottingham, as I prepared to do so, Peter, the schoolboy, and his understudy arrived at the stage door with me to check for any mail. When I moved to the stairs Peter asked me where I was going. 'To check the stage,' I replied. Peter, a fifteen-year-old who hadn't yet learned to worry about anything, said 'Oh leave it, Scotch' (he always called me Scotch) – 'where the hell could it be?' (he swore like a trooper, under the impression he sounded grown-up). Before I could stop them, he and the understudy had seized both my hands and rushed me out of the theatre and down the street, and refused to let me return.

That night the stage manager informed us we had a new call-boy who had never done the job before, and that after our first call for first entrances we had to watch all our own cues. She would keep him right for all first calls – after that we must be on our guard. Now these were theatres with no Tannoy equipment and we resigned ourselves to spending most of our time in the wings after the first promised call. It was going to be a long week, we felt, as we went upstairs to put on our make-up.

As this stage manager went up like a light if you doubted her efficiency, I didn't dare put in an appearance before her instructions to the new boy to call me, but it seemed a very long time between finishing my make-up and hearing the knock on the door. I tried to tell myself I was simply nervous because I knew the lad was new. I opened the door, to see Peter's understudy strolling along the corridor. I knew he watched the schoolboy's performance every night to help him with his own understudy rehearsals, and never left until Peter came off. And Peter's exit was almost the cue for my entrance! Not wishing to believe the lurching fear in my stomach, I called out to Robert, 'Where's Peter?' 'Just behind me,' he answered carelessly. I couldn't *believe* he wasn't as alarmed as I was to find me sitting in my dressing room at such a moment. It took years for me to learn that actors bother about nobody's worries but their own. Seizing my school satchel and my hat, I leaped along the corridor yelling, 'If Peter's off, then I'm off too!' It was then I realized I hadn't the slightest idea where the stage was, and whether I'd have to dive under it, go round the back, go upstairs, or what. 'Where's the stage,' I yelled, as I ran. Dressing-room doors opened and heads popped out It was like a French farce.

'That way,' and fingers pointed as I ran.

'Can I go round the back,' I yelled.

'No.' It would have to be a dive down and a race up then. Oh God! I'd be sacked. The other actors would be on stage with not a line to say until I entered.

I flung the study door open and launched myself at the table, gasping for breath. Colin Gordon fixed me with an eye blazing with scorn, and strolled towards me. Silently I tried to tell him with my eyes that I was sorry. I was sorry. Oh I was sorry. On his first speech, he spat, accidentally, straight into my eye. It stung like vitriol, took some of my mascara with it, and rolled down my cheek in a slow black tear!

I had to go to all three actors later and apologize, but the stage manager apologized too, and confirmed that I had been told not to move until I'd had my first call. By chance, our company manager was sitting out front that night watching the performance, and he comforted me considerably by saying that the fact that I was playing a schoolgirl had saved the day, because my gulping and gasping for breath was so natural, and my speech so jerky that I sounded like a gawky school kid in the presence of masters, so that the late entrance hadn't even been noticed. It helped a little, but after that experience I never again took the slightest notice of the feelings of stage managers, and I got myself down to my entrance position well ahead of my cue for the remainder of my stage life.

It was at Wimbledon that I learned the misery of playing to practically empty seats after weeks of full houses. It was the week running up to Easter, a notoriously quiet week in the theatre, and the few who did turn up rattled like peas in a pod in that vast auditorium. Margaret inspired us all. 'Let's just consider this a lovely, lovely rehearsal all for ourselves,' she would say. 'Let's enjoy ourselves, and if we do, then those people out front will enjoy themselves too.' Wonderful psychology. We threw ourselves into our performance, ignoring the empty seats, and went at such a gallop that the brave souls who had been prepared for a half-dead performance rose to cheer us at the end. Clever Margaret. Replacing the fatigue which is induced by trying to please an unresponsive house with the zest which comes from arousing an enthusiastic handful.

I learned something else at Wimbledon. As I called out 'Good night' on the Thursday after the performance, I added as usual, 'See you tomorrow.' To be met by the words, 'See you Saturday.' I stared, thinking the first actor who replied had forgotten the day of the week. 'What happened to Friday?' I laughed, expecting to see him slapping his leg and saying, 'Oh of course, I meant, see you Friday.' To my surprise, I was met with a disbelieving stare.

'It's Holy Day,' he said.

'Holy Day?' I echoed. 'What's Holy Day?' They couldn't believe their ears, those others now out on the landing on their way home.

At last Myles said, 'Well, I knew you Scots were heathens, but I thought even you celebrated Holy Day.'

'Holy Day – the Friday before Easter Monday.'

'Oh!' I said. 'You mean Good Friday. Of course I know about Good Friday, but that's not a holiday in Scotland.'

They were aghast. I was delighted. For if I hadn't said 'See you tomorrow' I'd have gone all the way to Wimbledon, only to find a shut theatre. And I was also rather relieved not to have to pretend it was another rehearsal for ourselves. Nervous as I was of facing a West End audience and top critics on Easter Monday, I longed to get it over with, and to play to full houses again.

Sandy was coming down for Easter, and it was so lucky that we were opening on a holiday Monday, for he would be able to see the show and get the overnight train back to Glasgow and his job. We would have to follow a different routine if the show were a success, which we felt in our bones it must be. He would come down to London every alternate week-end, which was the most we could manage financially between us, and as he worked alternate Saturdays it fitted well with his own arrangements. His ex-RAF pal, Van, a public schoolboy who was now continuing his studies to be a doctor, was also in London and they'd spend their evenings together on Saturdays while I was at the theatre; they'd served together in the Middle East and it was a wonderful opportunity to renew their friendship. Van's people were in Rhodesia, so he too was at a loose end.

In spite of the tour, we had another dress rehearsal on the Monday at the Apollo and, unbelievably, more notes on our performances. How could anyone expect *any* of us to change a single nuance at this stage of the play?, I wondered. But a West End opening is charged with an electricity which sends sparks in all directions, and there was a compulsion to polish and perfect while there was yet time, before we faced our most critical audience.

The theatre pulsed with excitement. The buzz of talk and laughter could be heard even upstairs in our dressing rooms. Telegrams were arriving every minute. There were half a dozen pinned to the notice board from the author, the management, other managements, other authors – names which I'd only ever seen on billboards or on playbills, now all interested in our success. To my surprise I had quite a collection myself. I had never expected such interest. From the Pantheon Club, from the family, from neighbours, from the McFlannels, and I pinned them all round my mirror in time-honoured fashion and hoped fervently that I'd be worthy of all that enthusiasm, and that all the 'Good lucks' would support me in the following two and a half hours.

Then it was curtain up, and I stood poised outside the study door, praying, as always, that I might do my best. A roar of laughter greeted the swift sweeping away of the sports gear into Colin Gordon's waiting arms, and a warm happiness spread through me from head to toe. As I skipped lightly off stage at the end of the scene, the audience broke into enthusiastic applause. I'd got my 'round' – and from a West End audience! Oh what a *marvellous* feeling. I had tried to forget that Sandy was out front. Now I was so glad that he was there, and hoped he might feel that all the separation had been worth while to see me take my place on the same stage which held the incomparable Margaret Rutherford.

At the end of the second act we could still hear the laughter of the audience two floors up, and they were so exhausted that the first five minutes or so of the third act were played to an almost silent house. Our hearts plunged to our boots. We hadn't realized we had left them too limp to respond. Then it surged forth again, and in the end we took almost a dozen curtains.

Visitors erupted into the dressing rooms. 'It was *marvellous*, darlings. You'll run for *years*.' 'We couldn't even move to go to the bar, we had laughed so much.' 'A tonic. Just what we needed in these post-war dreary days of rationing.' Sandy stood at the back, a dazed expression in his eyes.

'Did you like it?' I asked him.

'It was great,' he said. He took me back to Clapham, then went for his train.

The newspapers were rapturous in their praise. 'This play will fill the Apollo for a long long time,' was the general opinion. 'How long?' I wondered. Poor Sandy, having to face that journey every second Friday night. And then my heart burst with joy as I read again that every critic had actually liked my performance enough to mention it – even with Margaret Rutherford and her magnificent comedy to fill their eyes and ears. They wrote that they found me 'engaging', 'effervescent', 'irrepressible', 'amusing', 'cheeky', 'mischievous', and they *all* enjoyed the play on the name 'Barbara Cahoun *not* spelt Colquhoun'.

The last of the bruising I had suffered in losing ITMA vanished under the soothing words of the top critics of the day. Barbara Cahoun waved Tattie a cheerful good-bye.

7

Now began what Sandy described as my 'rat-run' to the Apollo six days a week for two whole years. I couldn't have believed there were enough people in the entire country to fill a theatre to see the same play for such a long long time, but London has always been a mecca for tourists, and our play was a 'must' for every holidaymaker who set foot in the capital. School holidays found us packed to the roof with youngsters and their parents having a day in London as a treat, and they added tremendous zest to our playing with their yells of laughter, and uninhibited screams of delight at finding school-teachers on stage embroiled in fast and furious farce.

It was a painful adjustment to have to return to more sophisticated adult audiences at the end of the holidays, but houses continued to be packed, and 'House Full' notices stood outside the theatre most nights. I found this announcement so impressive that I used to walk round by the front of the theatre every night, just to see with my own eyes that we were still packing them in.

My 'rat-run', once worked out, never altered for the entire length of the play. Tube to Leicester Square, cross the road and through the little alleyway which led to Gerard Street. Along Gerard Street and up Macclesfield Street into Shaftesbury Avenue, thence round by the Globe front entrance, a quick look at the 'House Full' board outside our theatre, then double back to the side street and through the stage door. At first I was very puzzled as to why I seemed to see the same ladies every night loitering on the edge of the pavements and in the doorways in Gerard Street and Macclesfield Street. Always in ones, and sometimes even calling to one another from a distance of about a dozen yards. Why couldn't they move over to speak more comfortably?, I wondered. They looked as if they were waiting for someone, but surely they couldn't be kept standing around *every* day at the same time? They gave me a keen glance at first as I raced past them on my way to the theatre, and I was actually on nodding terms with one or two of them. And then I read a little paragraph in an evening paper which deplored the blatant street-walking permitted in the West End of London, which was offensive to tourists, and not punished nearly heavily enough in the courts! My heart gave a great lurch. I was on nodding terms with prostitutes!

From that moment on, I wore not a scrap of make-up as I fled along the familiar route, in case anyone might mistake my purpose, and I hardly dared lift my eyes to the heavily made-up 'Ladies of the Night' now that I knew them for what they were.

Another terrible thought suddenly struck me. Was it possible that I had once been mistaken for such a 'lady' myself? I stopped dead in my tracks as I remembered the incident. I had become friends with a girl who had been auditioning with me at Alexandra Palace for some TV work, a foreign girl who had her own flat and who invited me to pop in for coffee one morning. I had to be there at eleven o' clock, she said, but when I arrived she was still in dressing gown and slippers, which I thought slightly inhospitable since I had been invited after all. When I went into the bathroom I was amazed to find at least a dozen pairs of beautiful silk stockings hanging from the pulley. Where had she got them? Where had she managed to find such treasures, and where the precious coupons? Somehow I didn't like to ask. It was a mystery, for I had certainly never found so much as a single pair of real silk stockings in all post-war London, and was still darning the pair Jimmy had brought me from the spoils of war.

This girl and I took singing lessons from a teacher whom she knew, so I saw her pretty often, and I decided she must be very rich, for she had no obvious source of income, and yet she wore lovely clothes, even had a little mink tie which I greatly coveted, and she also found the money to feed a beautiful little white poodle, as I discovered when I visited her flat. One evening, when I'd visited her for tea, she decided to walk with me to the corner newsagent's to see if there were any replies to something she had been advertising, and she left me outside with the poodle. I stood at the edge of the pavement, not wanting to lassoo anybody's legs with the lead as the animal frisked around me, and I gazed about me with interest, as this was a part of London I didn't know very well. A man came over, very well dressed, raised his hat politely and asked me if I were waiting for anyone. 'Oh yes,' I assured him, in the normal friendly Glasgow fashion. He looked at me and I looked at him, and he seemed to be waiting for me to say something else. I wondered if he was lost, and wanted directions.

'I don't live in this part of London,' I said helpfully, 'I'm just waiting for Marie. She's inside the shop. This is her dog.' It was the daftest sort of conversation with a complete stranger, and for some unfathomable reason the man seemed completely baffled. He was no more bewildered than I was, for if he was lost why couldn't he say so? And why had he come over to me in the first place?

I smiled amiably and said, 'I'll just go and see what's

keeping Marie,' and although I had been warned not to bring the dog into the shop, as the owner didn't like it, I walked boldly in, poodle and all, and told her that a man seemed to want to speak about something and maybe she would know, as she lived around here. She gave me a strange look, took the poodle, and walked me to the Tube. And it was that poodle which now made sense of the whole episode, for one or two of those 'ladies' in Gerard Street stood with poodles! No wonder that man was puzzled. He had known the code language. I hadn't. The wrong response had thrown him completely off balance, and my innocence had been its own protection. But I blushed for shame at the memory.

I once saw Marie much much later, long after we had drifted apart, and in fact during the run of *The Happiest Days*. We were always being asked to sell flags for various charities, the organizers working on the theory that well-known actresses would be more likely to meet with a generous response than other unknown females. I was standing outside St James's Church in Piccadilly when I was galvanized by the sight of Marie, dripping in mink (full-length coat this time), with a plump, very elderly gentleman in tow, also immaculately turned out. Rich and fat and ancient. Clearly, a sugar daddy if ever I saw one. Marie let him go on a few yards, then murmured something and turned back to me with the note he had handed to her. As she pushed it into the tin, and accepted the flag I pinned into her gorgeous coat, she gave me a mischievous glance.

'Still working hard for a living, Molly?' she asked.

'How about you?' I asked, after telling her about the play. 'Are you still singing?'

She looked briefly at her elderly Romeo. 'Only for my supper,' she said. She gave my hand a little squeeze and was gone. Now that my eyes were open a little to the ways of

London, I could see so clearly that Marie's interest in singing was purely as a little pastime. Her real profession was the oldest one.

Meeting her again like this reminded me, with a stab, of all those silk stockings hanging in her bathroom, and of how I had lost my precious pair brought home to me by brother-in-law Jimmy from the war. It happened while we were rehearsing *The Happiest Days of your Life* at the Haymarket Theatre. Incidentally, I was fascinated by our being allowed to work in a real theatre like this for our rehearsals, to give us the dimensions and atmosphere of a proper stage. The stage manager of the Haymarket company cleared the props away nightly, which I thought must have been a great nuisance, but, of course, it ensured that no vital item was missing for the following performance if the rehearsing company had picked up anything as a substitute prop for their own play, and didn't put it back where it ought to be.

I was delighted to have this empty prop table to perch on while waiting for my cue, and from which I could see everything that went on on stage. I was sitting up on this table, painstakingly darning my one and only pair of pure silk stockings with the tiniest stitches I could manage, for I always liked to have a little sewing on hand to pass the long waits between scenes. Now and again I couldn't resist a loving glance at my brand new handbag. I'd bought it the previous Sunday morning at Petticoat Lane for £7, my first new handbag since the war, and quite the finest leather I'd ever possessed. There was a fortune stowed in the purse, a whole £14, because when I'd gone home for a few days for Christmas everybody in Glasgow had given me cash instead of presents, telling me I'd be able to take advantage of the bargains at the New Year London sales and get the very latest in London style from those big shops in Oxford Street. I'd meant to put the £14 in the bank till I wanted to spend it, but with our 10 a.m. rehearsals and our late finish each day I hadn't been able to get there. So I'd brought my Post Office Savings Book and would put the cash in there when we broke for lunch.

I could hear my cue coming up, and I popped the silk stockings and scissors inside the bag before going on for my short scene. There wasn't another thing on the table, for it was almost lunchtime, and the other members of the company had bags and coats beside them ready to sprint for the stage door the moment the producer said 'Break for lunch'. My back was to the prop table while I was playing my scene, and the moment I finished I turned to pick up my bag and put down my script in its place. It wasn't there! Without even pausing to think of the implication of my words, I called out in anguish, 'Somebody has stolen my handbag.' There was a moment of stunned silence, then a babble of voices, some annoyed, some helpful.

'Don't be silly, nobody could have *stolen* anything!' 'You've probably forgotten where you left it.' 'It has maybe fallen down. Let's look for it. Where did you have it last?'

Dully, I told them that I had left it there, on the prop table before I went on to do my scene. Now, apart from £1 taken from my pocket as I stood in the Co-operative to pay the bill when I had been a wee girl, I'd never had anything stolen from me, but I just knew in my bones that somebody had pinched my new handbag. It hadn't fallen anywhere. It couldn't have. There was no place for it to fall. The backstage floor was clean as a whistle. And everyone else had been either on stage or sitting in the stalls. Nobody could have knocked it down, least of all me.

I asked the stage manager to send for the police, but he refused, and said it was tantamount to accusing someone.

With beating heart and near to tears, but still obstinately logical, I whispered, 'I'm not accusing anyone. But the fact remains that my handbag has gone, and somebody must have taken it. The police should start looking for whoever took it, without delay.'

He wouldn't listen, and just put a hand in his pocket and lent me five shillings to buy my lunch, and cover my fare home, for I hadn't a bean. Everything was in the handbag. As I tried to swallow a pie with dry throat, and dabbed my tear-filled eyes, I kept remembering the other things in the bag. My return ticket to Glasgow. My best fountain pen. My diary. How would I *ever* remember all those agents' addresses and telephone numbers? I gave a gasp as I remembered my keys were also lost, not only the keys for my digs but also for our house in Glasgow, and *both* addresses were in my diary so the thief knew where he could go to rob me of the rest of my possessions! Was there no end to the villainy this man could do to me? There wasn't. For my Savings Book was gone too. I gave a sob, as I remembered two almost irreplaceable items. My ration book containing my sweetie coupons and my clothing coupons. Without those it would be impossible to buy either the chocolate which I loved, or anything to boost my meagre wardrobe.

'*Why* wasn't the stage manager more worried?' I demanded passionately of Viola Lyel, who played Miss Gossage in the play, and who was seated opposite me in the restaurant.

She looked at me sadly, 'I once read a marvellous little story, Molly,' she said, 'about a girl who lost her luggage at a railway terminal, and she kept rushing about trying to get porters and station staff to interest themselves in her dilemma. Nobody took her seriously, assuring her it would surely turn up. It didn't. It had been stolen. And when she sat, bewildered, crying, she asked an old lady who came to comfort her why people could be so callous and so indifferent to her loss. The old lady had taken her hand and said gently, "Well, you see, it wasn't *their* luggage."' Viola looked at me with her sympathetic troubled gaze and said, 'You see, Molly, it wasn't *his* bag.' I never forgot those words.

When we got back to the theatre we found that a thorough search of the place had revealed no handbag, as I knew it wouldn't, and the police were summoned from Savile Row. Even in the midst of my misery I was conscious of a *frisson* of excitement at the mere idea of policeman from that famous station rushing to my rescue. Once they'd taken details of the handbag and its contents, they said, 'Why weren't we sent for at once? The thief has had two hours to make his escape.'

'Because,' I said, near tears again, 'the stage manager wouldn't let me do it. He said it was tantamount to accusing somebody in the company.' I was far too truthful to be tactful!

They had a word with the stage manager, patted me on the shoulder and told me to try not to worry, but with so many deserters on the run it was doubtful if I'd ever see the contents of my handbag again. However, it was just possible that I'd recover both bag and Savings Book, for with £14 in cash, plus at least the fiver he'd get for the coupons, it was doubtful if he'd take the risk of trying to sell the bag or of using my Savings Book, for both would be traceable and might lead to his being caught.

I poured out all my sorrow to Miss Chree when I got home that night, and she comforted me with tea and hot buttered toast, and a sound cursing of the dastardly malefactor who had 'robbed the orphan'. Miss Chree could always be relied upon for a good heart-warming biblical phrase. And Mrs Parker, my landlady, promised to light a candle to St Anthony, who was apparently the saint who helped to find lost things. What my grannie would have said to a Roman Catholic saint being called upon to help, I didn't like to think, but I hadn't the heart to refuse such a kindly offer.

And then, most baffling moment of all, came a telephone call on the Sunday morning from, of all people, the manager of the P. & O. shipping offices in Trafalgar Square. I could hardly believe my ears when, having ascertained that I was Molly Weir, he said, 'Have you lost a handbag?'

'I have,' I shouted down the telephone, 'but how did you know?' It appeared that on the Saturday night, a night of torrential rain which made him reluctant to leave his cosy fireside to investigate, one of the office cleaners had reported having found a lady's black leather handbag tucked behind the cistern in one of their lavatories.

Having instructed her to leave it in his office until he came over next day to investigate, he hadn't thought there was any urgency until the weather improved! He regretted now, on hearing the full extent of my loss, that he hadn't let me know at once. We arranged that I would call at his office and collect it on my way to rehearsal on Monday. St Anthony had turned up trumps, except that there wasn't so much as a penny in my handbag, and all the coupons had gone too. But the diary was there, he assured me, and the Savings Book, and my keys. As I rejoiced over what had been left, I remembered my silk stockings. No, there were no stockings, and no scissors. Clearly the thief knew such things were scarce in post-war London.

Next day, when I went in to collect the handbag from the P. & O. offices, the manager and I tried to work out what had happened. We came to the conclusion that the thief, probably a deserter as the police had guessed, had been watching the stage door and realized that it was a rehearsing company which was using the theatre. Relying on the stage doorkeeper not recognizing the faces of all the members of the visiting company, he must simply have slipped past him in the hope that Friday would be pay day and we might have some cash about us which he could pick up. Seeing my bag on the empty table, he had probably thrust it under his jacket, strolled out of the stage door, then crossed Trafalgar Square to the P. & O. offices. He no doubt knew the layout there, and had gone up the outer stair leading to the top offices, which were being painted and whose lavatories were left open for the workmen's comfort; he had obviously found enough money and coupons to make a possible sale of the bag and fradulent use of my Savings Book not worth the risk, and had pocketed cash and coupons and thrust the bag behind the cistern. And there it was eventually found by the cleaner. When I offered to leave her ten shillings for her honesty, the manager wouldn't hear of it. 'Not at all, young lady,' he said, 'you've lost enough without another ten shillings. I feel very guilty for not having taken the trouble to brave the storm on Saturday and for leaving you to worry another night unnecessarily, and if there is any reward called for, I'll see to it.' It was very fair of him, and quite restored my faith in humanity.

But that episode engrained itself in my heart, and never again would I let my handbag out of my sight, even when visiting a private house. Indeed, it was thanks to this caution that only a few years back, when I was working for Jimmy Logan at his Metropole Theatre in a play *Beneath the Wee Red Lums* and a sneak thief emptied everybody's purses during our final notes two hours before curtain up on the first night, when we were all on stage and dressing rooms left unguarded, mine was the only purse not rifled. I had taken it on to the stage with me! In the words of far-off Vere Foster, just as 'A burnt child fears the fire', so does the victim of a thief's predatory fingers take precautions against future attacks.

The final touch of drama connected with the affair came when I went to the Ministry of Food's offices in Clapham to ask for replacement sweet and clothing coupons. They took details of what had happened and then told me I'd have to wait for a month. This was a useful deterrent against those who simply carelessly lost their books, or tried to trick the authorities into letting them have spare coupons undeservedly. I, who had genuinely been robbed, was outraged. 'What,' I cried with furious denunciation of this lack of fair play, 'have I to suffer all that loss without even a sweetie to cheer me up? You can check with Savile Row and they will confirm my handbag was reported stolen, *and* with the manager of P. & O. shipping who will confirm that when found all cash and coupons were missing.'

The supervisor had emerged from his inner office at the sound of my voice. Clearly, he recognized the tone of truth when he heard it. 'Give her her sweet coupons,' he said, 'and explain the position over clothing coupons.' I didn't mind waiting a week or so for the latter, so long as they arrived eventually. I laughed aloud on being given a whole month's sweetie coupons – they hadn't even asked me if I'd used any, and I had! Out of disaster had come sweetness. I couldn't wait to cross the road to buy some chocolate to take back to the digs, and enjoy it over a cup of tea with Miss Chree.

If the winter had been so harsh that I was forced to wear my cashmere under my blouse, the summer was so tropical that it was torture to have to change out of a cool sun-dress and don thick navy-blue bloomers, gym slip and blazer and sling a satchel of books over my shoulder for my part as the schoolgirl. And, of course, long black thick stockings and heavy flat shoes. I began to appreciate the miseries of a long run when you wore precisely the same clothes as your stage character, whatever the temperatures outside. The performances after matinées were especially ghastly. The heat generated by the early performances never seemed to dissipate, and when one stepped on stage in the evening, the air hit one like a blast furnace. And the terrors of a long run were beginning to manifest themselves. For the first two or three months, changing audiences and a deepening and developing of the performances kept us all on our toes. Then familiarity began to breed, not contempt, but an entire repertoire of nervous traumas.

The first thing to happen was a terrible fear of 'drying', theatre jargon for the mind going blank, and instead of confidently assuming that the right words would spring to the lips as they had done for months, one began to think ahead and make the very thing one feared, actually happen. Or at least *almost* happen, for just as the stomach was turning itself inside out with frenzied terror, and disaster loomed, the mouth suddenly found the familiar sentence and only cold rivulets of perspiration betrayed the hidden apprehension.

This might go on for weeks until one settled down, and then a new hazard would present itself. If a fellow-actor altered so much as a word in a sentence, the jolt was so unexpected that hysterical laughter threatened to engulf one. And this is the very worst thing that can happen to any actor playing in farce. It must be played with utter serious-ness, for if the actor is obviously enjoying himself, then the audience is not, for conviction has gone straight out of the window.

And that was the worst form my own nerves took. I never *wanted* to laugh, but the slightest deviation from the script or from the expected reaction sent waves of hysteria over my head and down my arms and legs until I fairly shook with suppressed giggles. I used actually to take pins on to the stage at one point, and stick them down my fingernails to stop me laughing, for the author often visited the theatre and grew livid if he suspected we were spoiling his play with our unseemly mirth. I never showed anything outwardly, I'm happy to say, but it took a terrible toll of my health and my weight dwindled to around six stones. I wasn't the only one, of course. We never discussed our particular traumas with one another, for we were far too busy conquering our own to wish to worry anyone else with fears they may not have entertained on their own account!

Practical jokes were another nightmare. I was much too frightened to indulge in them myself, but that didn't stop other braver souls from involving me in their capers. I remember one night Myles Eason, who played the young handsome master, was feeling a bit bored and decided to enliven the evening. He had been doing a great deal of sunbathing and was brown as toast all over. When I made my entrance, he, with his back to the audience but facing me, swiftly opened his blazer with a movement of his hands which were thrust deep into both pockets. On his bare torso he had painted, in vivid grease-paints, two enormous eyes on his chest, a nose underneath, and a huge mouth across his navel. I stopped dead, stared, tried to open my mouth to say my lines, couldn't get a word out, and raced out the door on the other side, without a cue for anyone! As I was playing a schoolgirl, the audience suspected nothing, but the other actors were livid.

On another occasion, Joyce Barbour, who had taken over from Margaret Rutherford temporarily while Margaret was on holiday, hissed out of the side of her mouth 'Elephant's ears' because I had concealed my ear-rings with thin pieces of sticking plaster, as removing them daily for the performances was making them tender, and I was trying this trick to see if I needn't take them out for each performance. Again, the unexpectedness of the remark and her sheer control in being able to make such a comment during the show paralysed me, and again I was unable to get a word out. I headed for the French windows, and fell on the stairs sobbing with laughter. Joyce was furious, because again nobody got a cue, and she said later, 'There's no use trying to get a bit of fun at Molly's expense – you might as well gag her, for not a damn cue does she give!' That was the end of anyone trying to 'dry me up'. And it wasn't even a deliberate counter-attack on my part. I was simply unable to fool about on stage and still give a performance. I'm the same today.

Audiences, too, provided their own nightmarish behaviour. We had a hysterical woman in the front row one night who threw up her hands and screamed every time Margaret Rutherford appeared, and in the interval Margaret had to request that she be moved further back in the stalls or she would simply be unable to continue with her performance. Poor Margaret had to have sal volatile, and have her face and wrists dabbed with eau-de-Cologne to calm her down!

Another night, everybody warned me *en route* for my entrance to be prepared for a man with an unnerving laugh. So many people seriously warned me that by the time I wrenched the door open I was a nervous wreck. Sure enough, on my first line there was the sound like that of a whistling kettle, ending in a gasping gurgle, and I clenched my fists and willed myself not to dissolve in laughter or run off the stage. Unfortunately, this man thought I was the funniest character on stage, and my every line was greeted with this whistling shriek. The poor chap had been a war victim and the air in his throat was coming through an implanted device, but at the end of that Saturday night I was so distraught that I vowed that I was going to give up the part, for I'd drop dead if I had to go through another such performance. 'Go home and have a nice quiet Sunday,' I was advised by the others, 'and you'll be right as rain by Monday.' Well, I didn't drop dead and I didn't give up the part, but I had nightmares for quite a while afterwards.

During that year the 'new look' came out, and although I stubbornly refused to part with my old clothes merely because they were the wrong length, remembering the precious coupons which had been spent on acquiring them, I just had to subscribe to current fashion and drop the hem-line to mid-calf on the dress I had made for the theatrical garden party. I'd never been to such an affair in my life, and I felt very excited when I was told that our company would be running the skittles stall, that I'd have a badge of office, be an official helper, and in fact be one of the 'stars' on show. A wee star right enough, but fully entitled to take my place among the constellation.

The dressmaker delivered my dress the night before the party, and as far as I was concerned, that was the start of the affair. I thought it was quite lovely. Chalk white with a brilliant design in red and blue flowers, square neck demurely frilled, full new-length skirt, in fact exactly my idea of what a garden-party dress ought to look like.

A crafty piece of buying at a Bond Street sale had yielded an 'Ascot' cherry suède bag 'marked down' from a fabulous sum to something within my reach. I had rejuvenated last year's straw with a spray of cornflowers, poppies and marguerites, and couldn't help laughing as I remembered Grannie's switching from winter cherry trimming to summer flowers to ring the changes with her one hat, to make it suitable for all seasons. I was following in her footsteps, all right. I washed my white lace gloves, cleaned my white shoes, and felt that if only the weather behaved itself, I might be a credit to Scotland and *The Happiest Days of your Life*. I didn't even consider an alternative outfit in the event of rain. It just wasn't going to rain. Anyway, I hadn't anything else in my wardrobe remotely suitable for such an occasion.

Came the morning, and with it grey skies and an ominous wind. I ignored the elements as I filled in my morning with writing, tidying, having a bath and then a little light lunch, and I never even glanced out of the window as I arrayed myself in my delicious finery. Just as I applied the last flick of powder to my nose, the rains came – not in drops but in sheets, and with them a wind which shook the trees and rattled every window in the house.

I looked questioningly at my other self in the mirror. Change into something sensible, like my old suit? Not on your life. The public were paying 7s. 6d. to see the stars, and they weren't going to see me in old tweeds and a felt hat. Come flu, come pneumonia, I intended to be seen in my frothy ensemble if I died for my vanity. I seized a scarf, jacket and raincoat, squared my shoulders and flew downstairs into the rain before common sense could assert itself and make me change my mind.

A policeman was directing the stars' cars as I walked through humbly on my own two feet and took my place in the queue for my official badge which cost me a shilling. I was a bit surprised at this. I thought they'd have supplied it for nothing.

When I looked around me I felt so thankful I'd kept on my finery. It was a second Ascot. I had an impression of flowing veils, frothy hats, grey toppers, taffetas, chiffon, lace, all blending in an overpowering effect of elegance. And, best of all, the sun had come out.

Sightseers thronged the other side of the rope barrier trying to identify their favourites, and I wasn't above doing this myself, although I was on the right side of the rope.

Our little boy understudy, who ran over to me, couldn't recognize a single personality because they seemed to him so different from their screen or stage selves.

I pointed out Rosamund John, Dickie Attenborough, Sheila Sim and Mrs Michael Wilding, who were close by, and he was greatly impressed when I spoke to Kathleen Harrison and Mrs Stewart Granger, whom I knew.

A churning of cameras announced the arrival of Noël Coward, who strode to the microphone to declare the party open, and we all flew to our appointed places to take up our duties.

We'd scarcely reached our skittles stall when Margaret Lockwood and Noël Coward appeared, with cameras, in hot pursuit, and were photographed in the act of throwing the balls. I managed to coax Raymond Massey to 'have a go', and he was so mad at missing the first three shots, he risked another bob just to prove he could hit something. He did, and nearly liquidated our manager!

I popped across to see Tommy Handley, who instantly demanded half a crown from me and made me a member of the Fiddlers' Union, handing me a little red plastic fiddle to prove it. He was highly amused when I also demanded an autograph and I was allowed to go to the head of the queue, seeing I was 'Tattie'.

Turning round, I came face to face with Noël Coward and Elspeth March, and to my joy was introduced to the man whose genius I had admired from the moment I'd read *Private Lives*. When I told him that reading this had cured me of flu, he laughed with amusement and added, when Elspeth told him that I was now with Margaret Rutherford at the Apollo and was the cheeky schoolgirl he'd seen in the play, 'Well done, Scotty.' I was practically airborne with delight after this encounter, and flew back to our skittles stall on winged feet, and persuaded people to part with their shillings with such enthusiasm that we soon had a long queue waiting for balls and autographs.

One man, buried under a mountain of umbrellas, bags, and coats belonging to his womenfolk, informed me solemnly that mine was the prettiest dress in the garden party. The very nicest part of this compliment was that he was so serious about it, as though he had truly given the matter great thought, and I felt I could take a chance and believe him!

A little boy in front of us at the tea bar turned to his mother and said, in very puzzled tones, 'Mummy, how can you tell the film stars from the ordinary people?' Through the laughter which followed, I said, 'You can't, son, except that by this time they're all a bit more haggard than anybody else from signing hundreds of autographs and posing for pictures.'

In the ripple which followed this, somebody said, 'Oh, it's wee Tattie, isn't it?' and the next few minutes saw me selling autographs at sixpence a time. It was a shilling for Margaret Rutherford's, so I thought half-price for mine was pretty fair, and all the money raised was for charity anyway.

A bus called for us at five-thirty and we were carried back to the bright lights and the evening performance, and although we ought to have been exhausted, somehow we weren't, and we even forgot all the traumas of the long run after the stimulus of our afternoon's activities. The crowning moment for me came when somebody handed me a copy of the evening paper, and there I was standing in the background between Noël Coward and Margaret Lockwood! I hadn't realized that I was within camera range when they'd been throwing their skittles at our stall. If I'd known, I might even have risked charging a bob for those autographs!

Miss Chree had to be told every detail when I got home from the theatre that night, and she had the tea ready as soon as she heard my feet on the stairs. The incident she enjoyed most, because it demonstrated the good manners of well-brought-up children, was when I told her of Robert Morley's visit to our stall, with a handsome little boy in the swankiest camel coat I'd ever seen worn by a child. The wee boy spent two whole shillings without scoring a hit, and when I said sympathetically, 'Och never mind, you can try again next year. I'll see you then,' he said, brightening, 'Oh yes, I will. I'll see you next year.' I watched his little figure striding away, when he stopped dead and clapped a hand to his mouth.

Running back to me, he gazed at me seriously and said, 'Oh I'm so sorry. I shan't be here next year. I'll be in Australia.' I thought it both touching and hilarious that anyone so young should know exactly where he would be a whole year ahead, and be so conscientious in correcting a promise he found he couldn't keep. That was Sheridan Morley, and I never dreamed the day would dawn when he and I would both address ladies' luncheon clubs, and both share the same attitude of not accepting too many such engagements in case we wouldn't be good enough or they might not like us. In my case, sheer fright counselled caution, but, remembering the sincere and truthful little boy I'd met all those years before at the one and only theatrical garden party I'd ever attended, I felt quite sure it was sensitivity and consideration which made him assess his talents so modestly.

8

We were very strategically placed at the Apollo dressing rooms to see first-night openings at the Globe Theatre next door, and the first star-studded one after own own happened to be *Medea,* starring my friend Eileen Herlie, whom I had last worked with in the Pantheon Club in Glasgow. Eileen had preceded me to London and had worked out at the Lyric, Hammersmith, in her husband's company, but this was her first major role in a big West End production. Greek tragedy in London was a far cry from *The Desert Song* in Glasgow and the one-act play where Eileen as the wife of the retiring shipworker says, when consulted as to whether her husband would like a clock or a watch as his parting gift, 'Ah think Wattie wid rether hiv doos.'

My heart beat for her as I watched the glittering West End first-night audience arrive. I may say I was hanging out of my dressing-room window to see all this, a practice which would have been severely frowned on by the management if anybody had caught sight of me. Between getting my own make-up on, and getting dressed for my performance, I kept rushing back and forth to the window, alerted by Peter the schoolboy and his understudy, who kept me advised as to what was happening. They were glad of any diversion to offset the boredom of our long run, and we cooed over each arrival as enthusiastically as any of the crowds lining the pavements. Noël Coward, Diana Wynyard, Coral Browne, Margaret Rawlings, Richard Attenborough, Jack Buchanan, Jack Hawkins, John Mills, in fact everybody who wasn't working in the theatre himself on that night.

We became so absorbed that we practically forgot our own curtain, and I had to shoo Peter out to get made up and dressed or he'd miss his entrance. Eileen told me later that she had been absolutely exhausted with emotion at the end of the second act, and had sat and stared at herself in the mirror, wondering how she could get through the third act. She said it was then she realized how right Binkie Beaumont had been when he told her the greatest asset any tragedienne could have was physical stamina, and that at times it was needed more than talent. This was such a moment. She gave herself a pep talk. 'They're all out there waiting for you to fall flat on your face,' she told herself, 'so go out and show them!' And she did. When the whole of our company went to one of their Saturday matinées later in the run, I saw what she meant. Indeed the whole play was such stark relentless tragedy that we, watching, were utterly whacked by the time we tottered out at five o' clock to have tea and go through our own performances. How Eileen endured having to *do* it eight times a week was beyond me.

I used to join Eileen for tea after our Wednesday matinées in her star dressing room, and rejoice in the luxury of having tea brought to us on a tray. She hardly ate a thing, but I carried round my sandwiches and cake, and enjoyed sharing the splendour of the No. 1 dressing room, and chatting in unguarded Glasgow patois of all the goings-on in both theatres. She had settled into the run by this time and had learned to conserve her energies and her emotions, but, having been longer in top show business than I, she envied me my uncomplicated approach to the whole thing, and sighed when she said, 'Ah this is the best time for you, Molly, when it's all excitement and fun. Wait till it becomes routine, and you simply pass the day waiting for the curtain to go up. That's when it's a nightmare.' I was later to appreciate her words to the full, but then they were just meaningless chatter, or at least sentiments which would never apply to me.

Sandy enjoyed hearing all these tales when he came down each alternate week-end, and although the days between may have dragged a bit for him, he was busy enough with job, house and garden to keep him from wearying, and intrigued by his jaunts around the capital every fortnight. His ex-RAF colleague, with whom he'd served in Cyprus and the Middle East, was also in London studying for his doctor's degree, and they renewed their friendship, glad of one another's company, for both were at a loose end on Saturdays, Sandy because I was in the theatre with two shows to do, and Van because his people lived in Rhodesia and he had few friends outside the college. They went to all the cricket matches and all the theatres, and in the end I found digs for Van near me in Clapham, so he was able to pop round and join us for supper or sometimes for tea on a Sunday if the weather was poor and we couldn't go sight-seeing. It was lovely seeing London like a tourist, because we had no home duties to keep us house-bound at week-ends, and as Sandy said, 'We'll probably find that if we ever live down here, we'll not see a tenth as much as we're doing now, because we're so free.' Events later proved him dead right. We visited the Tower, the Houses of Parliament, the Tate Gallery, the National Gallery, Hampton Court, Windsor, Madame Tussaud's, in fact all the 'musts' of the tourist's London.

Not that we were contemplating moving to London just then, but, like me, Sandy was baffled that *The Happiest*

Days was still playing to packed houses week after week, with no signs of this state of affairs coming to an end. When he was able to stay over one Monday because it was a public holiday in Scotland, he came round to the stage door to collect me before going for the night train. The stage-doorkeeper never having seen me for more than a moment or two in my ordinary clothes, and having gained the impression from my school outfit and my running around back-stage with Peter, the real schoolboy, that I was a juvenile, was distinctly sceptical when Sandy asked him to tell Molly Weir that her husband was waiting for her. He rang upstairs and said to me, with a chuckle, 'There's a guy down here who says he's your husband, Molly. I told him to get lost, but he insists I speak to you.'

'He probably *is* my husband,' I said. 'Is his name Sandy?' George practically collapsed on the spot, and shook his head in disbelief each time I raced past his cubicle on my way to the stage.

'Her with a husband,' he would say, 'I just don't believe it!'

I was very impressed with all the theatre customs, and the strict observance of all superstitions. No whistling in the dressing rooms. No mention of the play *Macbeth* or the tiniest quote from it. No real flowers on the stage. And, a nice and unexpected touch, a little party on-stage after every hundredth performance, with champagne and toasts. Like every true Scot, it only needed the sight of such gala bottles to set me bursting into song and Margaret Rutherford used to say, mischievously, 'One look at a champagne cork, and Molly starts to sing.' It was a never-failing source of wonder to me that the English could be so douce in their pleasures, with not a cheer out of them to mark a joyous celebration.

The only trial to me at this time were the understudies.

With no duties or responsibilities, and everybody in radiant health, they were bored to tears. Unfortunately I had to share a dressing room with them, and was subject to all their noise, their tea-making, gossip, and occasional snide comments. I begged to have a dressing room to myself, or with another working actress who would be sensitive to the demands of the performance, but it was no good. I was smilingly informed it was quite impossible, there wasn't a corner anywhere, although I mutinously observed that the stage management each had a room to themselves, although they hardly ever had time to sit in it. It was bad enough when we were all reasonably fresh at the start of the run, but as time went on, and we all grew overtired, and had colds, and other ailments, it became one of the hardest pin-pricks to endure, and made me vow that if ever I had any influence in theatre regulations, I'd make it a rule that performers never had to share with non-performers.

Actually I got on very well with all three understudies, it was just this room-sharing which was a nuisance. Maria, my Russian understudy, struck me as being very sophisticated, and I couldn't understand why she was occupying this comparatively lowly position in the company. Peter, the schoolboy, used to attend understudy rehearsals just for the joy of hearing her utter my lines in her bored, oh-so-English upper-class voice, which made it seem like a different part after my robust Scottish accent.

She was a white Russian aristocrat whose grandparents had escaped to England at the time of the revolution, and she had been educated at the best English schools.

Maria held a special fascination for me, for not only was she the first Russian I'd ever met, but her father was part of the terrible history of Russia in the thirties, having been murdered in Siberia during the years of terror which followed the revolution.

Highly intelligent and a complete extrovert, she was both fascinating and maddening.

I once visited her flat and it was quite clear to me that nobody in that hilarious household had the slightest idea of humble housework. Up to a dozen milk bottles, containing milk in varying degrees of sourness, were ranged along the mantelpiece. To make cheese? I wondered. The table displayed a bible, a pair of long black gloves, and a bowl of beetroot, as though set by a stage manager, and the sink was full of tea-leaves.

The doors of the wardrobes were tied with silk stockings to stop the contents spilling out, and tea-packing cases stood everywhere, with clothes and books stuffed inside as though they'd arrived from Russia that week!

When I walked into the unlocked bathroom a lady was lying in the bath and languidly lifted a foot to soap it, never even turning her head to see who had come in. When I retreated in confusion, I bumped into a man who apologized, and who then walked over to the table, ate some of the beetroot and left. To this day I've no idea who he was, and nobody seemed to bother about his identity when I told them of the incident, any more than they bothered that I had seen the lady of the house stark naked.

I started to stammer an apology to Maria, and said my own mother would have had a fit if I'd seen her without her clothes on, just as I would have almost died of shame if I had been similarly exposed. Maria stared at me, baffled. 'Do you mean to say if your head was cut off, your own mother wouldn't recognize your body?' she asked in tones of such genuine amazement that my embarrassment dissolved in peals of laughter at such a macabre picture.

It was such an alien environment to me that I was quite hypnotized. But I couldn't endure the domestic clutter, and set to and washed all the milk bottles, having unstopped the sink first to get rid of the tea-leaves and other debris. Maria was enchanted and the whole household thought I was so clever, knowing what to do! I was suddenly reminded of a Glasgow friend who married a very indulgent man and who left all unpleasant tasks for him to do when he got home from work. When I commented on this she gave me a wink and said, 'Play daft, and you'll get everything done for you.'

With this to strengthen my resolve, it was easy for me to resist the temptation to succumb to future attempts to get get me back to this colourful 'Crime and Punishment' household to clear their kitchen confusion. After all, as Grannie would have said, they'd have to learn some time that a house didn't clean itself, and the more it was put off, the harder it would be.

Maria knew everybody. When celebrities visited London, there she was at the cocktail parties or receptions to welcome them. Tennessee Williams had only to appear in London for the opening of his new play, and Maria was along at the Savoy next morning having breakfast with him! The speed of such friendships took my breath away, and it was a revelation to me of the loneliness of famous people in a strange city that such instant rapport was possible.

But when she brought delicious American goodies to the dressing room, she also brought the maestro's dirty socks and shirts which she had generously offered to wash for him! Throwing them into the basin, she said to me, carelessly, 'You wash those, Scotch' (she always called me this, in fact many of the company did). 'You know how to do those things much better than I.' Throwing them neatly back at her, so that I could wash my hands at the basin before going on stage, I smiled sweetly and said, 'No, Maria, *you* got the food parcels. *You* do the washing.' She laughed. It was a try-on which hadn't succeeded, but she bore me no ill-will. See what I mean about Russian understudies?

But she did involve me in one mad adventure which almost got me the sack, for I had no idea I was doing anything wrong. Among her many colourful friends and acquaintances was an English milord. He was now ill in a West End nursing home and she brooded as to how she could cheer him up, and no doubt make a memorable impression at the same time. 'I know what we'll do,' she announced, a wide grin lighting her vivid face. 'We'll go to see him after the matinée.'

'We?' I echoed. 'What have I to do with it?'

Shouting with laughter at her brilliant inspiration, she informed me we'd both keep on our school uniforms (she had one too, as understudy), take a taxi from the stage door and go to the nursing home. There I was to pretend (in broken English, if you please) that we were Oncle Jean's nieces from Paris, that we had only one day in London, and that we passionately wished to see him to thank him for our lovely birthday presents.

'Maria we can't do it,' I protested feebly, for the idea had such a daft ring about it that it was somehow appealing.

She saw I was tickled by her inventiveness and hugged me. 'We can *easily* do it, Scotch. I've heard you imitate Yvonne Arnaud and I know you can speak broken English like a French girl. I'll be the one who speaks no English at all, so I'll stay dumb, for I can't speak "broken" anything.'

This flattery went to my head.

We took the taxi, which she'd ordered by telephone, and I couldn't understand why she was so anxious that nobody in the theatre should see us leave. We reached the posh nursing home, rang the bell and were shown into a waiting room. In halting English, keeping my eyes firmly off Maria, I explained we were Oncle Jean's nieces from Paris, ' 'ere for jus' one day, an' we weesh *so* much we speak wiz heem, to sank heem for our so-belle birthday geefts.' The nurse looked at us so sympathetically my stomach turned over with the weight of my deceit, and with a 'Wait here' she dashed off, and returned with the matron. The matron!

I had to say it all over again for matron, and the repetition was worse than finding courage to make my original speech. However, she suspected nothing, and we were shown up to Oncle Jean's private room where we found him sitting up in bed wide-eyed, wondering who on earth to expect.

We stood side by side by the end of his bed until the matron left, and gazed solemnly at him. He gazed back, his eyes going from one face to the other, in a complete daze of perplexity. Maria couldn't keep it up a moment longer, and burst into shrieks of laughter and threw herself on him, arms round his neck. It's a wonder he didn't burst his stitches with the shock!

As he hadn't a clue who I was, Maria explained my part in the practical joke, and we all had tea, which made a delicious change from our dressing-room sandwiches, while he got over the surprise of our visit. It had certainly brightened the normal routine!

During the conversation he happened to mention that he didn't know how he was going to cope with the mountain of mail which had accumulated during his stay in the nursing home. Maria turned to him, beaming, magic solutions provided as though she were the Genie of the Lamp. 'Oh, *that's* all right, Jean,' she said, without a word of consultation with me, 'Scotch Moll will help you. She's a shorthand and typing expert. She can come to your flat and take notes and bring them back next day.' The cheek of it!

When Jean wondered if he could let it lie until he got home, because some of the correspondence *was* pretty urgent, I said, 'Well, I'm certainly not coming back *here* to take notes. I couldn't face that matron again in my ordinary clothes, after that act we've just done for her benefit. She'd probably shoot me.'

Maria was enchanted to infer from this that I *would* go to his flat, and as he seemed such a young, helpless milord, I said I would.

When we got back to the theatre and emerged from our taxi, breathless with laughter over the success of our impersonation, the stage manager happened to be standing in the doorway. She jumped as if she'd been stung, and fixed us both with an outraged eye.

'Have you two been out in your *stage clothes*?' she demanded, although it was perfectly obvious that we had. 'If the management saw you, you'd both be sacked on the spot,' she cried. 'It's absolutely forbidden to cross the threshold of the stage door into the street in your theatre clothes.' She couldn't have frothed at the mouth more if we'd run down Shaftesbury Avenue stark naked.

I stared at her in bewilderment, and then at Maria. I saw from her expression that she had known this all along. *That* was why she'd been so anxious not to be seen when we'd left in our taxi in our gym slips. The monkey! Now that the adventure had been successfully accomplished, she didn't care a button. 'Oh, don't be such an old fusspot,' she said. 'Nobody saw us. And unless you tell them, nobody will know we've been out in our school uniforms.' I must say I admired her ability to cut right through to the heart of the matter, without the sort of argument I'd have got into if I'd tried to explain. My expression of dismay must have been convincing proof of my innocence of the management rule, for I was merely told not to let it happen again.

Maria never troubled her head with the tiresome aftermath of her behaviour. She was like Peter Pan, showing unabashed delight in being able to provide solutions to problems. But it was I who had to trail from my Clapham digs to Chelsea several times a week, take down dull notes of business deals, type them out the following morning between my usual chores of washing, ironing and shopping and other writing, and deliver them to Chelsea again on my way to the theatre.

I was glad when it was all over, but Oncle Jean was flatteringly complimentary about my speed and efficiency and thought it a terrible waste that I neglected all that secretarial expertise for the treadmill of saying the same lines eight times a week in the theatre. He wasn't surprised, he said, to learn I'd trained as a secretary, for he hadn't had anyone half so good!

How could he know I was completely stage-struck and had gladly exchanged my typewriter in Glasgow for grease-paints and Shaftesbury Avenue.

The next time he asked my help it was to type out invitations for his wedding. Not to Maria, alas, which I had romantically dreamed of – to a member of the English aristocracy.

I refused. I'd seen inside his lovely flat, which had been the most interesting part of the whole experience, and I simply couldn't endure all that travelling back and forward again. I knew too that inevitably I'd be roped in to cope with all the other correspondence involved in a society wedding, and, remembering the frenzied activity of my own much simpler nuptials, felt I'd never be fit for my theatre performances on top of this secretarial assistance to make his wedding bells ring smoothly and merrily.

Maria's mother was very impressed and amused by my loyalty to my dreams for her daughter, in turning down this opportunity of earning a little pocket money, and I felt mean when I heard her praise me for something which hadn't really been the mainspring for my refusal. It was my sense of responsibility towards the theatre which had bade me say 'No'. Not but what the pocket money wouldn't have been very useful, for the West End salary at that time was £10 a week and even with my frugal ways I had to budget very carefully to 'owe not any man'.

But amazingly, in the end, in the very words of all those romances devoured by Grannie and me in *My Weekly*, Maria married her milord and they lived happily ever after, and had two beautiful daughters.

She is now a milady, and I see pictures of her opening fêtes, going to the races, at first nights at the theatre, and greeting Tennessee Williams on his frequent visits to London, for their friendship stood the test of time and has lasted through the years. I wonder if she remembers the dirty socks and soiled shirts I refused to wash? If she doesn't and she reads these words, I know she'll throw her head back in that characteristic way I remember so well, and her whole face will light with laughter. She was a character, and in time I came to feel quite privileged that I'd shared a dressing room with someone who had lived a life which was the very stuff of story books.

During that summer we were going through one of the 'cold war' phases with the Russians, and one night I stopped on the stairs to talk to Myles at the end of the second act. Wee Peter, the schoolboy, came rushing up to us. 'The iron curtain has come down,' he panted. I went white with shock. Well, the blood drained from my heart and I *must* have changed colour. I was always fully aware of the political scene. 'What?' I cried, 'have they declared war?' Peter looked at me as if I was mad.

'Have *who* declared war?' he said impatiently. 'It's the iron curtain. It's come down.'

'Well, it must be the Russians then,' I said, 'they're trying to frighten us.'

'Scotch,' he said slowly and clearly, as if talking to a half-wit, 'the iron curtain in the theatre has come down. The *fire* curtain. And it's stuck. It won't go up. The hydraulic thing has broken, and they're trying to wind it up by hand, but it won't budge.'

The relief was so great that I burst out laughing, not realizing the implication for the poor audience, left at the end of act two, not knowing how the play would finish, their evening's entertainment abruptly ended. And the poor front-of-the-house staff having to cope with replacement tickets for those who wanted them, or money back for those who didn't. For the curtain had indeed come down for the night. It was a curious feeling of anticlimax to be out in the street in daylight by nine o'clock, and because I was so used to working all evening I couldn't think of a thing to do with this gift of an hour, and simply went back to my digs. I was on a treadmill, all right, when a break in routine could find me so unimaginative.

For Sandy's two-week summer break we took rooms in a guest house in Leigh-on-Sea, and I travelled up and down to the theatre daily. It wasn't a success. I kept being terrified I'd miss my train, or it would stick in a tunnel, as it had one night when Duggie Ives, who was playing the porter and who lived at Leigh-on-Sea, had been thus marooned. Margaret's husband, Stringer Davis, had had to play the porter that night, and I had nightmares every time I remembered him with his two scripts, one at either side of the stage, so that he could check his lines before each entrance. Stringer, who had had years in repertory theatre, wasn't too worried about having to make sure of his lines like this, but to me, watching him, it was an actor's nightmare come true, when in dreams you find yourself about to go on stage and can't remember a word of the play.

We never saw the sea properly for the whole nine days

we stayed at Leigh. The tides were wrong, and there were what looked like miles of mud. The sun was coy too, and to crown it all, Sandy got shellfish poisoning. That was the end. We called it a day and returned to Clapham.

I put Sandy on a light bland diet, and by the time he had to return to Glasgow he was right as rain. When he could speak about food without shuddering he made me laugh by telling me that on that day of the shellfish poisoning, when I'd left early for my matinée, he had decided to dine at the little café on the so-called beach. The entire menu had been composed of fish dishes, and the wee woman ahead of him had gazed at it mournfully and then said, in lugubrious tones, 'Don't want no more fish,' before turning away sadly and drifting into the rain. Ever afterwards that phrase was quoted by either of us when faced with too much of any-thing, 'Don't want no more pies, or mutton, or whatever,' and somehow it expressed perfectly the whole dreariness of that ill-chosen holiday.

The next event which broke the routine of the 'rat-run' to the theatre was the death of Dame Lillian Braithwaite, that lovely actress who, with Joan Harben's mother, Mary Jerrold, made *Arsenic and Old Lace* such a memorable theatrical occasion. A notice pinned to the green baize board near our stage door informed us of the time and place where the memorial service was to be held, and I, always eager to savour the complete experience of being a working member of the theatrical profession, determined to be there.

When I reached All Souls' Church in Langham Place there was the usual crowd of sightseers which always seems to gather in London when anything is afoot, no matter what the hour of day, and they recognized their favourites with excited whispers as the stars passed into the dimness of the church. Discreet reporters asked for names in hushed tones, and jotted them down with a reverent air, as though wishing to impress on all of us that they knew their place on this solemn occasion. How polite the world was then, and how we took such tactful behaviour for granted.

The church was packed to capacity. Everyone who was anyone in the theatre seemed bent on making a personal appearance, and I was surrounded by well-known faces. A hymn sheet was handed to me by Bobby Howes, and I was suddenly reminded, rather appropriately considering the present occasion, of the first time I had seen him in a musical in Glasgow when he had sung 'Got a date with an angel'. The voice had been so sweet, so gentle and so appealing, that the entire theatre had held its breath, not to miss a single note. Leslie Henson, with whom I'd worked on my very first TV show, showed me to my seat, and later John Clements handed across a plate for my offering, which I saw was to help the Theatrical Ladies' Guild and the Actors' Church Union. I hadn't realized church collections could go to charities, and thought the ones chosen for this occasion most appropriate.

Everybody had an uneasy air, and seemed afraid to smile in case their lip movement might be mistaken for levity. Nobody spoke. It was as though, having been given no lines by the author, they were bereft of words. When I murmured to a fellow-actor that there were more people present than I'd anticipated, several people turned and frowned, although I'd spoken very softly.

In spite of a fairly extensive repertoire of hymns and hymn tunes gained in primary, Sunday school, bible class and church, the ones on the sheet quite unknown to me. I gathered the rest of the congregation were equally ignorant, for the singing was terrible. The piping voices of choir members emphasized that they were a mere handful, and underlined the dumbness of the hundreds standing clutching their hymn sheets, not a note coming from any of them. It was a relief when we could sit down again.

Leslie Banks read beautifully the chapter from the Corinthians, and one felt there ought to be a round for him at the end.

Mark Hambourg played 'The Sunken Cathedral' by Debussy, and it seemed strange to me to hear a piano in church. But for the few brief moments as he played the church borrowed the atmosphere of the concert hall, and people relaxed, back in their own environment for a little.

Then came the parson, with his rolling sentiments about Dame Lillian. I couldn't see her somehow in the saintly creature he drew for us. I kept seeing her as she went fastidiously about the business of murder in *Arsenic and Old Lace*, or as she poured scorn on matinée audiences and their noisy tea trays. I couldn't help remembering the delicious exchange between her and Agate, when he complimented her on being the second loveliest actress in the room, and she instantly responded, 'That is a great compliment from the second-best critic in London!' A smart riposte, if ever I heard one, for the doyen of theatre critics of the day. Dame Lillian herself would have been the first to deprecate too fulsome tributes to her virtues, and to relish appreciation of her wit and sparkle. I expect we all had our own memories, for there was a strangely contemplative silence as the parson's even voice flowed over us.

John Gielgud then read in vibrant lovely tones from the *Book of Revelation*, and there wasn't a sound as he descended from the pulpit to take his place among us again. Everybody seemed moved by the beautiful words.

Then came the ordeal of another hymn, the collection, and it was all over.

The lady at the end of the row refused to budge till she had seen all the stars pass, so we were forced to stand too until she consented to let us go. Famous personalities of stage and screen moved in a steady stream, but their expressions had been smoothed to such a uniform and becoming gravity, that I found it hard to recognize them in this unaccustomed quiet pose.

Evelyn Laye gave me a dazzling smile, no doubt mistaking me for somebody important, and I smiled sweetly back, trying to look as if I was, and I included her husband Frank Lawton in my greeting.

The crowds were waiting for us to come out, and I caught the overflow of their enthusiastic smiles and murmurs because of the very famous half-dozen stars who were immediately ahead of me. I tried to pretend to myself it was because I looked to them like a successful actress, but their puzzled smiles made it all too clear that I was an unknown among that galaxy.

After the theatre that night, when I was having my bedtime cup of tea with Miss Chree, I started to tell her with some excitement of the memorial service, and I showed her the little sheet with the order of service and the famous speakers' names. To my amazement, she sprang to her feet, shaking with indignation when she came to John Gielgud's name, and, pointing to it she said in a voice of doom, 'I don't know how you could bear to sit in the house of the Lord, with fornicators reading the lesson!'

I was quite bewildered. I had seen the word in the bible, but didn't entirely know what it meant. Indeed, I had to look up a dictionary when I left her.

Knowing how Myles Eason adored everything connected with Miss Chree and her Scottish ways, and slightly amused myself by her reaction which I felt was strange and unjust, I told Myles what she had said. He roared with laughter, and with the tears of merriment streaming down his cheeks he said, 'Poor John. Oh, poor John.'

Next night, to my horror he informed me that he had told John Gielgud what Miss Chree had said about him. 'Myles,' I gasped, 'you didn't. How could you? What did he say?' I fully expected to hear he was coming to the stage door to hit me for repeating such a calumny. Myles laughed again. 'He fell about. He thought it was the funniest thing he had heard. He'll dine out on it for years, and so will I.'

I felt I'd never understand the English, not if I lived among them for a thousand years.

The year jogged on, and in no time at all, it seemed, it would soon be Christmas. We'd only have a day off to mark the event, and extra matinées would be played to fit in all the youngsters who were to be brought to see us as their special holiday theatre treat. Sandy didn't get Christmas off, but would come down at New Year, seeing the English hadn't yet learned the civilized custom of taking the day off on New Year's Day.

Miss Chree was working, but Sandy had brought a bottle so we could bring in the New Year in time-honoured fashion, and when I got home from the theatre we got out the glasses and the shortbread and cake, all ready to toast 'absent friends'. And then we discovered we hadn't a corkscrew, and we needed one for our particular bottle. 'Mr Finch is sure to have one,' I said. He lived with his wife directly underneath my room, and was on the stage management side of the business. He was the sole male in our feminine domain. So we went down, and he was so glad to see another man in the house and so starved of show business conversation that he kept us talking, talking, talking, for nearly an hour. It was freezing cold. I was standing right in front of the draughty door, and after the heat of the theatre I could feel the shivers running up and down my spine. But I was far too unsophisticated to say I was getting cold, and that my feet in their slippers were slowly resembling two blocks of ice. After our hot summer it was a perishing winter. And we all felt it. And there was a flu epidemic.

By the time we reached my bed-sitter my teeth were chattering, and it took two wee swigs from the Hogmanay bottle to warm me up, and I hoped I wouldn't catch cold from this episode. The following Wednesday, matinée day, I wakened with every bone in my body aching, and my head like a football. I've always been susceptible to the flu bug, but I refused to acknowledge the symptoms and decided I'd just pop along to the doctor to confirm that it was nothing more than a slight chill which was making me feel so grim. I wanted his assurance that it was safe to play the matinée. His waiting room was packed; I longed to ask to go ahead of my legitimate turn, for I was feeling more and more ill, but I just couldn't bring myself to utter the words. When I did get into the consulting room I explained that I was in a play in the West End, and would he confirm it was all right for me to do two shows, and that I hadn't flu. He was busy, and brief. He told me to get some tablets, busily writing out the prescription as he spoke, and I was to take two and would be all right, he was fairly sure.

When I got the tablets from the chemist I was terrified of the effect they might have, for we were all having another trauma over 'drying', and thought I'd leave them till bedtime. I got to the theatre, and happened to meet the company manager, and told him I wasn't feeling very well. 'Oh,' he laughed, 'old Dr Grease-paint will do the trick. You'll feel fine once you've got your make-up on.'

I didn't. I got through the first act in a dream. In the second act I came to the part in the play where I was supposed to put out my tongue and do a fierce grimace at Myles, because he was in love with the school-teacher on whom I'd a crush. I seemed to be speaking through a thick sheet of glass, and Myles' face was a very long way off. I knew I had to do something with my face, but couldn't think what it was. With a supreme effort, I wrinkled my nose slightly. I could see the surprised expression on Myles' face, and the next moment I'd run off, clutching my throat and tearing at my tie to get air. I collapsed at Stringer Davis's feet, where he was standing waiting for his cue, for he and I had a longish scene which should have followed almost immediately.

He took one look at me, realized the understudy would never be dressed in time, and he played the entire scene as though I were outside the French windows, repeating all my dialogue at second-hand. 'The little girl says . . . etc., etc.' and the audience suspected nothing. Stringer was always superb in an emergency. At any other time it was as much as one's life was worth to address a word to him as he waited to go on, for he was busy mouthing his words. But in emergency all his adrenalin rushed to his aid, and he coped brilliantly, remembering not only his own dialogue but all of mine.

At the end of the scene the manager came out in front of the curtain and announced that I had been taken ill, and that the part of Barbara would be played by the understudy for the rest of the performance. There was scattered sympathetic applause and a few tut-tuts, but by this time I was in Margaret's Rolls-Royce, chauffeur-driven, and was being taken back to Clapham. They had rung through to the landlady to have the room warm, and she, not at all used to Valor heaters because she had a coal fire, had lit both the gas fire *and* the Valor, but had turned up the Valor stove far too high. So that when I arrived, shivering and sweating by turns, the windows were wide open to the icy air, and you couldn't see across the room for black oily smuts!

Everybody in the house supplied hot-water bottles, and

although they were being kind, I longed for them all to go away and leave me to die in peace. Miss Chree was still away keeping house for her Persian family, and Mrs Finch and Mrs Parker made me endless cups of tea, but I couldn't get a bite of food down. Indeed, the first food I ate was when Miss Chree came back one afternoon and was horrified to find me so ill and with the slops still under the bed! As a good housekeeper, this outraged her more than anything. She came back that night, having raided the rich Persians' fridge, and brought me frozen raspberries and jelly, which she liberally covered with glucose. I can almost taste the beautiful fresh flavour of that luscious sweet as I write. It was the first moment since my collapse that I felt I might possibly live to tell the tale, and go back to the play again. When Miss Chree had listened to all the details she threw up a dramatic hand, 'All for the want of a corkscrew,' she said. For she was convinced, as I was, that it was that Hogmany chill which had made me vulnerable to the flu bug and which had led to my undoing. 'All for the want of a horse-shoe nail,' we both chanted, and I felt slightly better. She was always a tonic, was my splendid Miss Chree.

Recovery was extremely slow, for my temperature would come down in the morning, and go roaring up again at night till nightdress and sheets were saturated. Margaret Rutherford and Stringer visited me, and when she saw my white face Margaret drew in her breath in that marvellous hissing movement which convulsed audiences, but which touched me now to the heart, at the generosity of a leading lady of her quality taking the time to travel out to Clapham and climbing three flights of stairs to bring me a little comfort. She was like a fairy-tale character, with her beautiful, voluminous fine green tweed cape, with green velvet bonnet, tied in a huge bow under her chin. She and Stringer had brought flowers, and, most lavish gift of all, their egg ration, three beautiful brown eggs in a little basket. She rushed about tidying the room, while Stringer found a container for the eggs and a vase for the flowers, and I felt I was dreaming as I watched them. How could one ever forget such a kindly gesture, in the midst of a long taxing theatrical run, when every moment off stage was precious? I know I never could, and I treasured my friendship with her till the day she died. I like to feel I was able to return a little of it in the intervening years.

Sandy was appalled at my appearance when he arrived for the week-end, for now my face was festooned with ghastly herpes, those painful blisters I always took when my temperature was affected. I felt slightly better in myself, in spite of my looks, and on the Sunday at teatime, when he went out to the landing to fill the kettle, he suggested I switch on the radio to see if I could now stand the sound of it. It would reassure him that I was indeed better if I could, for he knew what a joy I found my little radio. He switched it on himself as he passed the table, and the first words I heard were, 'It is with regret we have to announce that Mr Thomas Handley collapsed and died late this afternoon.'

I shot bolt upright, dissolved into tears, and sobbed hysterically, 'Sandy, Tommy's dead.' He rushed into the room. His first thought was of my brother Tommy.

'How do you know?' he asked, thinking I was light-headed.

'The man on the wireless has just announced it.' It was the one and only time that Tommy had ever been announced as 'Thomas'. And it was the shock of this tragedy which was directly responsible for us moving to London.

9

It is no exaggeration to say that the entire nation was as shocked by Tommy Handley's death, as though it had been the death of a monarch. Three days before they'd heard his irreverent comedy crackling over the air, and now he was dead. They were stunned. They couldn't take it in. And when they did they were filled with grief. The BBC were thrown into a frenzy of activity, for in spite of all grief, the fact that the shows went out live meant something would have to be devised quickly to replace ITMA within four short days. The air was filled with tributes to Tommy. The newspapers printed his picture, and details of his death within heavy black bands.

I lay in my little room in Clapham, so ill with shock that the doctor pursed his lips and said that I must on no account think of attending any services for Tommy. The bereavement on top of the flu virus had not only knocked my slight recovery for six but had sent me right back to square one. When Francis Worsley rang me to tell me details of the cremation service I couldn't speak for tears, and Miss Chree had to take the phone and explain that I wouldn't be able to attend any of the services.

On the day of the funeral I listened to the radio, while all London came to a standstill. The streets were lined with Tommy's mourning public, six deep, and many wept unashamedly as they watched 'that man' take his last journey. They remembered, as we who worked with him remembered, how he had kept the nation laughing throughout the darkest days of the war. All those catch-phrases which somehow had a magic of their own to dispel gloom. 'This is Funf speaking'; 'Don't forget the diver'; 'After you, Claude. No, after you, Cecil'; 'Dirty postcards, sir? Very spicy, Oh crikey!'; 'A gin and tonic, suh? I don't mind if I do'; 'What *is* kissing, Papa?'; 'Can I do you now, sir?'; 'No cups outside'; '*Good* morning, nice day, I'll call again'. And so on, and so on, and into peacetime with the new catch-phrases: 'It's being so cheerful as keeps me going'; 'What's cacophony?'; 'Och you're daft'; 'Would you care for a sninch of puff?'; 'I'm all right now'.

Finished. Gone in that fatal fall as Tommy bent to pick up a collar-stud which had rolled under a piece of furniture, and never rose again.

When Joan Harben rang me later to tell me of what a shattering experience it had been to take part in the final tributes to Tommy, she said I would never have stood it in my poor state of health. She said the terrible communal grief was almost beyond enduring, and she was sure that never again would London see such a tribute to an entertainer. For he was, of course, much more than that. He was a symbol of defiance over the worst evil this country had had to bear for many a long year. And he was a symbol of the free world, and of victory.

My temperature continued to go up and down like a yo-yo, and when the local doctor was baffled, the theatre management sent me to Harley Street. I could hardly cross the specialist's room, I was so weak, and had to lean on the furniture as I made my way from the door to the chair. I was impressively sounded and examined all over, when it was pronounced that I was suffering from a type of pneumonia which needed complete rest. So there was no question of going back to the play until I had had a good long holiday. I was sure I'd never go back again, for with understudies who were a good deal nearer Barbara Cahoun's age than I was, I felt Tennents would be quite happy to see me go. I maybe didn't need the stamina Eileen Herlie required for her heavy Greek tragedy, but I certainly required to feel a lot more chirpy than I could see myself feeling in the foreseeable future if I were to go leaping around the Apollo in the part of the irrepressible schoolgirl.

Miss Chree helped me to pack, and I left £3 hidden in a wee drawer, on which she could draw if the intervals between jobs grew too worrying for her. I couldn't bear to think of her being without shillings for the meter, or the odd tin of peanut butter, and some coffee. I had to be terribly casual about this arrangement or she'd have been up in arms at once. I just murmured as she shut the taxi door, 'Oh, there's some loot in the top drawer of the dressing table if you fall upon evil days' (a biblical turn of phrase always robs words of offence), 'so help yourself – you can pay me back any time. But of course it may not be necessary.' And before she could protest, I was out of sight, waving to her before the taxi turned the corner and hid her from view.

We went through this charade each time I left Clapham for any length of time, and great was her rejoicing if she hadn't had to touch it. 'I didnae ha'e tae touch it, lassie,' she would shout happily, 'wasn't it *good*?' And then, one time when I came back, she said mournfully, 'I had to break into the insurance in the wee drawer.'

'Well, that's all right,' I said, 'that's what it was there for.' I refused to consider taking it back, for I'd had a few unexpected broadcasts to swell the kitty, but she insisted I take the little ring given to her many years before by Lady Astor when she had been staying in the north at a fine hotel where Miss Chree had gone as temporary housekeeper. It was gold, and it was Georgian, and I regarded it merely as held in my custody until I could safely hand it back to her. But it is still mine, although the little catch is now broken, and the gold worn thin as tissue paper. She just wouldn't have it otherwise.

Sandy was delighted to see me in our own home again, although dismayed by my obvious weakness and pallor. Glasgow wasn't exactly a health resort, for it was still in the grip of winter weather, but I was freed of the strain of eight shows a week, I was in our own comfortable bed, and there were coal fires, and a garden, and comfort everywhere. I had been asked to let the management know when I was fit enough to return, but each time I suggested I ought to be thinking of getting back to the Apollo, Sandy declared it was out of the question, I was still weak as a kitten. It was true. Walking up the hill from the bus, a hill I didn't even know *was* a hill when we'd first moved there, I was panting for breath, and having to stop every few yards to rest.

Telegrams began coming from London. '*When* are you coming back, darling Molly?' from Margaret and Stringer. 'Barbara, for goodness' sake, *please* hurry back, before I'm quite crippled,' this from Colin Gordon. I couldn't fathom what he meant, but it later transpired that my instinctive timing when I swept cricket gear off the table into his waiting arms had been replaced by the understudy's unpredictable swipe, which had sent rock-hard equipment straight into his stomach and other vital parts so violently he had been unable to straighten up for the rest of the first act! He had developed such a terror of this scene that it gave him nightmares. From the management came: 'May we know when we can expect you back, please? Very much looking forward to seeing you in the part again.' I felt quite flattered, as well as genuinely surprised that they wanted me.

'Well,' I said to Sandy, with a small chortle, 'it seems that part really is mine, after all.'

I had been off for a month by this time, but Sandy said I must take another week – at least. 'If you saw yourself crawling up that hill, you'd know you weren't ready,' he said. 'In fact, I've a good mind not to let you go back at all.' But he didn't really mean it. He had as much respect for a contract as I had, and knew I had to finish what I'd set out to do. So I sent a wire saying I'd back on Monday a week later.

I travelled back on the Sunday, still feeling as weak as water, and with no suspicion of the psychological hangover I'd experience when I went to play the schoolgirl again. It was ghastly. The moment I put on the uniform, I felt exactly as I had the night I had collapsed. My face felt icy and hot by turns, and my legs like rubber. I got through the first scene all right, and was rewarded by a blissful smile from Colin when I swished the cricket gear neatly into his outstretched arms. But when it came to the scene where I'd collapsed all those weeks ago I felt on the point of fainting. I stood on one side of the French windows waiting for my entrance, and opposite me stood Stringer and his 'wife', Betty Wolfe. Betty must have known how I felt, when she watched me panting for breath, and wiping the cold perspiration which ran down my forehead. Every experienced actor has to go through this after illness. She was and is a very sweet and gentle little actress, and she shocked me out of my terror by giving me the thumbs-up sign and mouthing, 'You're *bloody* good. You can do it. We've missed you so much. Go on, you're *bloody* good!' This expletive from the mouth of such a dear little lady galvanized me out of my introspective terror, as she had known it would, and the next moment I was on stage cheeking Myles, rushing for my adored teacher, before screwing up my face and sticking out an impudent tongue at Myles. I exited to a roar of laughter; it was over, for that night at least.

But it took me a very long time to get strong again, and the traumas came oftener and oftener after that. And when he came down for the next week-end Sandy announced that it just wasn't possible to risk my taking another dose of flu and having to lie in digs dependent on landlady's attentions or non-attentions, and he was going to start writing for jobs with a view to moving to London. I was horrified. 'Suppose this success is just a flash in the pan?' I said. 'Suppose they grow tired of me? Suppose I get no more work when this play is over, and I'll have taken you from your job, your friends, your golf, and your family, and you *know* you like Scotland better than England.' Sandy brushed all argument aside. Now that Ma was dead, the strongest link had been broken, and if *The Happiest Days* was going to run for ever it was high time he was down here with me. I was overcome with guilt in case I'd have brought him down to an environment he would hate, and terrified my luck would run out and I'd have aided a move which would make him unhappy. And what would happen about our house in Glasgow, and how would we find one in the London area?

So he started taking the London newspapers and writing for jobs and I started getting little parts in films. In those days everybody in the theatre worked in films during the day, when they could, and their contracts stated they had to be away from the set by five-thirty at latest, to be in time for the theatre curtain at seven-thirty. Or if it was a seven o'clock curtain like ours, five o'clock was the deadline at the studios, for they were on the other side of London and a car could take a good hour to reach the West End. Mad as I was about films, it was a nightmare trying to get myself out of bed by 4.15 a.m. to be ready for a train around 5.20 a.m. which would connect with the studio bus right at the other end of the line, and which would get me to make-up for first morning call. I crawled about like a half-dead fly making tea and toast, and was sure I'd wake everybody in the house with my symphony of squeaking stairs and gasping breaths, but nobody stirred and the house stayed asleep.

When I opened the door, having slid the bolts aside very very carefully, I might have been the last creature alive in all London. The Grove was hushed and quiet, until an early car flashed into view, filled with miserable, disgruntled workmen, silently huddled into themselves.

The Tube at that time in the morning was transformed. A curious rushing noise had me completely puzzled, until I realized it was the machinery of the escalators, a sound unheard under the scurry of millions of feet in the daytime. It seemed incredible that not a whisper of this busy clanking had betrayed itself until now.

A coat lying on one of the benches turned out to be a workman half asleep. Like me, he was making sure of the first train, and he gave me a toothless grin, gums bare as a baby's. A chain of lights lit the tunnel where workmen were working right till the last minute, before the train was due. Everything seemed unreal, so still and bright, and only the whirring noise made by the lights and the distant thunder of the escalators broke this strange silence. I fell into a dreamy doze, wondering how it was that I who could never manage an appointment in town at 11 a.m. when I was working in the theatre, should be sitting waiting for a train at 5.25 a.m. And then, with a roar the train was in, and I was on my way.

From the word 'go' I loved everything about films. The cossetting. The being taken by the hand from wardrobe to make-up to set, always somebody to lead the way, to make sure precious time wasn't wasted. The 10 a.m. 'breakfast' break when I, who can never manage more than a slice of toast at home, was ravenous for the ham rolls and scalding tea from the big caravan-like truck.

And I especially loved my part in *Floodtide*, for it was based on George Blake's book about the shipyards, and was the first film I played in with Gordon Jackson and Molly Urquhart and the first time I met Jimmy Logan. I was playing a landlady, and Gordon and Jimmy were my lodgers, and 'make-up' pinned a bun on me to make me look suitably elderly. However, the director felt this wasn't enough to hide my youth. He said, to my amusement, 'Looking like that, the boys would never spend a minute away from their digs! Take her away and give her some wrinkles,' he commanded. So I had a few wrinkles added and my hair was dusted with special powder to disguise the sheen of my newly washed tresses. I've always had a passion for squeaky-clean hair, but it was the wrong passion to indulge for this particular part.

By the end of the day, though, I think the director had acquired a few wrinkles and grey hairs of his own, trying to put the scenes with Gordon, Jimmy and me 'in the can'.

The first scene was one in which Jimmy, my regular lodger, returned with a friend – Gordon – who was looking for digs. I was supposed to be a bit of a dragon, and had to stand back and sort of give him the once-over before deciding whether or not he was fit to be admitted to my house. Gordon was playing rather a timid type, nervous of meeting me for the first time.

As I've told elsewhere,[1] Gordon and I had worked to-gether in Glasgow, and were always in danger of exploding into laughter at the wrong places. The cameras went into action for the scene, and I started my slow appraisal,

1. *A Toe on the Ladder*

starting at his feet, and letting my eyes travel upwards. All went well till my gaze reached his face. Then as soon as our eyes met we both burst out laughing. Of course, Jimmy Logan joined in, and, anyway, by that time the scene was ruined.

The director shouted 'Cut', we composed our faces, we did the scene again – and the same thing happened.

We got worse and worse, until we were quite hysterical. 'Will we have a coffee break, Gordon?' the patient director said. 'The atmosphere is marvellous with you three Glaswegians, but we *do* have a film to make.'

'No,' said Gordon, nearly crying with vexation at himself, 'we won't stop for coffee. We *must* get over this.' It was all very well for Gordon saying this, but how was I to get over it? By this time Jimmy and I were hanging over the sink, holding our sides, despairing of finding any sort of calmness to play the scene.

And unknown to any of us the studio 'boss', J. Arthur Rank, was standing at the back watching, making a first-hand appraisal of a new technique which was being tried out for the first time in *Floodtide*.

While he had a word with our director, I took a long look round what was supposed to be my Glasgow tenement, and I was aghast to discover that the English idea was miles from the reality as I knew it. My wee kitchen mantelpiece held a huge five-valve radio, while a swanky open-fronted cupboard displayed a new hand-sewing machine. I took courage and explained to the director, who had now returned to the set, that the Glasgow mantelpieces in a house of that type were about eight inches deep and would never hold a large radio set, that we didn't go in for open-fronted cupboards, and that if I had a sewing machine it would be a treadle one.

'Props,' he shouted, 'remove sewing machine and radio.'

This little break was enough to steady us, and we shot the scene immediately afterwards without any trouble, although I had to hold my stomach absolutely rigid when I met Gordon's eyes or I'd have been off in a splutter of giggles again. Gordon confessed he too had been terrified till the moment was safely past.

The shooting went on till we came to a scene where I had to duck Jimmy Logan in a sink of soapy water, because he was being cheeky. The 'Glasgow' sink was a porcelain affair with a ruffled curtain draping it. 'Wait till you see the fun, Jimmy,' I whispered, as the cameras were being placed. 'Oh, Mr Director,' I called, 'that's not a Glasgow sink.' It was nearly the end of the day's shooting. Time was precious. And his face was a study as he took in this piece of information. He stared at all three of us, and then shook his fist in a fury, while we collapsed with laughter. 'Go to the devil,' he roared. 'Glasgow sink or no Glasgow sink, it stays in. It won't be in the picture, anyway, only Jimmy coming up soaking will be seen, so your artistic integrity is safe.' I really don't know how we had the nerve, or how that long-suffering director put up with us, but it was all the greatest fun, even if the long working day was exhausting.

Molly Urquhart and I were both appearing in the West End in plays, but her curtain went up at eight o'clock, whereas ours went up at seven, so she hadn't such a rush. The studio could only spare one car for the journey to town, and at the best of times this meant a dash for me, for they hated losing Molly Urquhart too soon, but hadn't the slightest compunction about keeping me a little later each day. One evening everything went against us. A very tricky scene just *had* to be completed, so that the set could be 'struck' and a new one built ready for next morning's shooting, and we were very late by the time it was safely 'in the can'. There was no time to change, and the bun was snatched off my head as I dashed past the make-up on my way to the studio exit. The minute we put our noses outside, our hearts rose to our mouths. It was foggy, and the car which was taking us to London bore the ominous words 'running in' in the rear window! So even if the fog lifted it couldn't go faster than the permitted 30 m.p.h. We both feared the worst!

In case of emergency, we always took our stage costumes to the studio each day, and now, with time running out, we decided we'd just have to change in the car, and then, if we were lucky enough to get to the theatre before the curtain rose, we'd at least have our stage clothes on. I began to shake when I realized Molly Urquhart too was worried about time, and *she* wasn't required till eight o'clock!

There we were, the two of us, wriggling out of our everyday clothes, and squirming around on the floor of the car below the level of the rear windows, praying that another car wouldn't coast alongside, or the driver turn round to see what on earth was going on. Suddenly, in spite of our anxiety, we both burst out laughing and the driver must have thought we'd gone crazy. It had struck both of us at the same time that, in the event of an accident or being stopped by the police, the driver would have quite a problem explaining how he came to have not one but two half-naked women in the back of his car!

As I leaped through the stage door, the curtain was going up and I knew I had exactly twenty minutes before my first entrance. I raced up the two flights of stairs, threw myself at the dressing table and slapped on my stage make-up, plaited my pigtails without anybody's help this time, stuck on my hat, tore my blazer from the hanger and put it on, threw my school-satchel round my shoulders, and was reaching for the door-handle when the call-boy arrived to say my cue was coming up!

I got a terrific telling off from the stage manager, who had seen me racing in as 'curtain up' was being called, for I hadn't even told her I was filming, and I ought to have been in at the 'half-hour' call, otherwise the understudy should have been alerted.

I got through the performance, but the whole experience so shattered me it took me about a fortnight to recover, and I felt so weak I thought I was taking flu again. It was this which decided me that as far as was humanly possible, I would never mix the two forms of entertainment again. It simply wasn't worth the nervous strain.

And yet I did accept another film part, in *Madeleine* for David Lean, because again it was based on a Glasgow tale. I was longing to play the part of Christina Haggerty, Madeleine's maid and go-between, but I didn't get it. Instead I was cast as the maid of Madeleine's parents, played by Barbara Everest and Leslie Banks. Ann Todd, whom I'd long admired, was playing the part of Madeleine.

I had a small but vital scene where I had to rush in with newspapers containing the news of Madeleine's acquittal. It was typical of David Lean's greatness as a director that even to this tiny episode he gave great thought as to how best it should be done. He was so nice and so enquiring that, feeling that I knew Glaswegians better than anybody else on that set, I stepped in where angels fear to tread and made a couple of suggestions as to how he might produce the effect he wanted. David Lean looked at me in astonishment. 'These are excellent ideas, Miss Weir,' he said, adding, 'You have unusual poise and attack for a small-part actress.'

I had the audacity to say to that great man, 'But I'm not a small-part actress. I'm only playing a small part for you!'

I waited for the heavens to fall, but Lean seemed highly

amused. Roaring with laughter, he said, 'I know what we'll do. We'll shoot the scene both ways you suggest. It's well worth it with somebody so interested as you.'

And that's exactly what we did.

When it was over, David Lean did something seldom seen in a studio. He walked over, kissed my cheek and congratulated me in front of the entire cast and crew. Considering he was the director who later made *The Bridge over the River Kwai* and *Lawrence of Arabia*, you will appreciate my delight over such a compliment. Even in those early days his quality was obvious to everyone who had the good luck to work with him.

Mind you, maybe it was his own joy that made him assess my wee contribution too kindly, for it was his first day on the set after his marriage to our star, Ann Todd. I have a vivid memory of her standing in her Madeleine costume, leaning gracefully against the set. She was absolutely radiant, her beautiful teeth flashing in the happiest of smiles as she received the congratulations of the rest of the cast on her marriage, and on her beauty in her lovely Madeleine gown. I was sorry my own little part was over. I'd have loved to have had more to do on that film and to have watched them all at work under Lean's brilliant direction.

And there were two hilarious little films I took while I was in the play, because they were what is technically termed 'on location', although the location in both cases was no further than Regent's Park in London, a bare ten minutes from the theatre, so no trouble about timetables at the end of the day's shooting.

The first one was shot in the zoo area, and I was with a wee five-year-old boy and Elsie Randolph. I couldn't get over working with this great star of the musical comedy days, whom I'd applauded from the gallery many a time and oft when she appeared at the Glasgow Alhambra with the one and only Jack Buchanan. Now here we were together on a drizzly morning sitting on a bench in the park, drinking coffee brought to us by a humane camera lad who saw how cold we were. The wee boy whimpered and wanted to go home, fed up with all the inevitable hanging about waiting for the light, so I took him over to a bear pit containing two huge bear cubs. Remembering that I'd seen a snippet in the newspapers that week about two bears having been christened by Jack and Daphne Barker, two entertainers very popular at that time, I took a chance and said to the wee boy, 'I know those two bears. Watch them when I call them.' He stopped whining while I called, 'Up, Jack. Up, Daphne.' Sure enough, the bears stood up on their hind legs, just as if I'd been a trainer! My guess had been right. They *had* been named after the stars. The wee boy was enchanted. There wasn't another squeak out of him all morning, although I had a terrible job avoiding his invitation to go round all the other animals and command them to stand on their hind legs!

The other film was in a mews not far from the park, and is memorable because I practically decapitated poor Leslie Dwyer, who was playing my husband. Knowing nothing about cars, I didn't realize the position his head must occupy to effect a certain repair, and I came blithely into shot and slammed the car door. He ducked just in time, but went white to the lips and clutched his head at the narrowness of his escape. 'Blimey,' he said, 'blimey, we've got a right one 'ere.' During our lunch break he took me all over the car and explained just what *not* to do when he was lying underneath the car repairing it, for he felt he had quite a lot of living to do if only I'd be careful. Incidentally, it was like the old church socials and Sunday School trips having our lunch handed to us in cardboard cake boxes, containing sausage rolls, sandwiches, and cakes. We could have crossed the road perfectly well and gone to a restaurant, but because 'location' means feeding the crew and actors, then a mobile canteen is brought into play and food distributed picnic-fashion.

This particular film is still being shown in Australia and other parts of our former far-flung Empire and I'm always getting little notes telling me people have seen it. I'm instantly transported to that little mews when I read those letters, and can see myself standing with the others eating sausage rolls from a cardboard box, London's traffic roaring past a few yards away, not even a chair to take the weight off one's feet. So much for the glamorous life of the film 'star' on location! But a whole lot of fun nevertheless.

This toehold on the film world was wonderfully reassuring, and an enjoyable fulfilment of the hopes with which I'd set out for London. I was in a play and I was doing films, so maybe I would continue to be able to find work when Sandy was fixed up with a situation in London and we moved south. I said the words, but I just couldn't *see* us settled in England. Home was Glasgow. Work was London. And never the twain seemed to meet in my mind.

But Sandy doggedly kept on writing, and fixing appointments to be interviewed on the alternate Saturdays he travelled to the capital. In those days people worked a five-and-a-half-day week, and Saturday morning interviews were not regarded as anything out of the ordinary. And at last, one Saturday, he returned from an interview and said he'd been offered a job with a firm of shipbrokers, and he was to start on an agreed day in May – about six weeks' ahead. He'd been in shipping all his life, apart from his RAF service in the war years, but hadn't touched the shipbroking side. He *had*, however, thanks to the booklet he'd picked up in Cambridge in our theatrical digs when I was touring,[2] taken a correspondence course and qualified as a shipbroker in case this qualification would be useful. Now his foresight had paid off. He would give in his notice, sell our house in Glasgow, put our goods and chattels into store until we could find a house in London, and establish ourselves in one place instead of living this separate existence and spending a fortune in travel. My stomach turned several somersaults, and I prayed to God we were doing the right thing.

And then a thought struck me. 'But I'll *have* to come up to look over my clothes, for there are heaps of things I won't want stuck in storage for an indefinite period, and heaps of things I won't want at all and ought to get rid of before the house is packed up.'

I was confident Tennents would allow me to take one Saturday off when the moment arrived, so I could travel overnight after Friday's performance, have Saturday and Sunday to go over my wardrobe and household goods, and return to London by overnight Sunday train, to be ready for Monday's performance. I never dreamed they would consider me such important 'box office' that permission would be denied.

Meantime Sandy had advertised our house, and it was sold almost at once. He said it was my 'blue room' which had captivated everyone who had come to look over the place. At that time, furnishing fashion in Glasgow tended to follow conventional colourings, greens, fawns and browns. But I had always had a great love of vibrant colour, and ignored the drab dullness which toned with dirty Glasgow weather; and I had chosen pale grey walls for our lounge, with a deep royal blue fitted carpet from wall to wall, apricot coverings for our chairs and settee, and apricot, blue and grey striped curtains. The sideboard and small

2. *A Toe on the Ladder*

tables were mahogany, and I must say it all looked very eye-catching. Sandy said the wives who came were so entranced with all this vivid colour, you'd have thought they were buying the contents, and so general was the enthusiasm for this room he began to have some respect for my talent as an interior decorator! This was a handsome admission, for at the time, he had thought I was raving mad! Pale grey paintwork in Glasgow – who had ever heard of such a thing?

Anyway, that was the house sold, and I sailed into Tennents' manager's office, all unsuspecting, and asked for the Saturday off, two weeks ahead, so that I could attend to my household tasks. I was quite unprepared for his reaction. He looked down at his nails, picked up a ruler, weighed it between his hands, then wiped the smile off my face with the words, 'I'm afraid it is quite impossible, Miss Weir. Saturday performances are extremely important in any theatre, even playing to packed houses all week as we are doing. It is a question of keeping faith with the public.' I opened my mouth to protest, but couldn't speak for the shaming tears which threatened to choke me. He rose in dismissal, 'I'm afraid your domestic responsibilities are no concern of ours. I'm sorry. We cannot allow you to go.'

I rang Sandy on the Sunday morning after the men had been to pack up the house, and I was in floods of tears. 'Oh, Sandy, not to see our house ever again as ours, and it's *months* since I was home. Not to walk all over it, and remember how we bought it and furnished it from our hard-won savings. Not to say good-bye to the neighbours. Not to have a last look at the garden. It's terrible.' Sandy tried to laugh me out of my sentimental weeping. 'You'd cry a lot harder if you could see the place right now,' he said. 'The men were rushing about like ants yesterday, and I don't know what they've done with half the stuff. I'm supposed to have it all marked for the storage people tomorrow, and I don't know where to start. You're far better where you are.'

Even at this distance in time I can hardly believe that the discipline of my life and of the theatre was strong enough to keep me from taking a farewell of our very first home, and deny me so much as a look at the people who would be living in our dream house, a house acquired after years of self-sacrifice and patient saving. Oh, I *ought* to have been there. But I wasn't and Sandy had to do the whole thing on his own. I was grieved when the new owners wheedled him into leaving a treasured set of bookshelves made by our brother-in-law, but it all turned out for the best, because, thanks to this concession, they agreed to our request to let us lift the gooseberry bushes which Ma had given to me as her last Christmas and birthday gifts before she died. I felt they were a living link and I wanted that wee bit of Scotland and my past to be with us in exile!

Sandy said everybody roundly cursed those gooseberry bushes on the train journey from Glasgow, and on the Underground between Euston and Clapham. Mrs Parker, too, wasn't very keen to have them in temporary quarters in her small strip of garden at the back of the house, although what harm she thought they would do I just don't know. I had to appeal to her better nature and to her Christian charity that it was only because they were a living link with my adored ma-in-law that I wanted them. They weren't just any old gooseberry bushes – they were special to me. I was exhausted by the time she agreed, and didn't mind the scratches I carried for days after helping Sandy to get them into the sticky London clay.

10

It was a strange, disoriented feeling being without a home, and Sandy certainly hated living in digs. We started looking for a house in real earnest as soon as he reached London. I had been looking for weeks, of course, studying the adverts in the London papers, visiting estate agents' offices, going to see houses in the daytime before my evening performances, and each week-end when Sandy wasn't with me.

The moment he arrived he started eliminating district after district in the evenings while I was at the theatre, and eventually we decided North London was for us. I'd spent many week-ends at the home of the little boy who played the schoolboy opposite me in the play, mainly because he'd driven his parents mad at the week-ends because he now felt too grown-up to play with his wee brother, and preferred the adult discussions and walks he had with me. So I knew I liked this side of town, which felt fresh and free and much more Scottish to me.

Amersham, where he lived, was too expensive for us, both as regards house prices and fares, and it seemed much too far away for daily travel, especially after the shorter distances travelled in Glasgow. So we came in a little nearer, and looked at Rickmansworth. Still too expensive. Then Moor Park. Still too expensive. We found Pinner properly one Sunday when we had several houses to see in Hatch End, and missed our train back to town. We'd always been intrigued by the designation 'Hatch End for Pinner,' and of course I'd also seen the name Pinner on the station when Peter and I flashed through *en route* for Amersham on Saturday nights. 'Pinner can't be too far from here, Sandy,' I said, when we realized we'd have an hour to wait for a train, 'let's see if we can walk to it, and have a look round.' So we started on our fateful stroll. We seemed to go on and on, and eventually outside a cemetery, where in the future I was to be asked many times by strangers the same question that I now put to a passing stranger, I stopped and said, 'Are we far from Pinner?'

'Just walk forward about two hundred yards and you'll see it,' was the reassuring reply. We did, and we came to the top of the prettiest High Street I had seen, a Norman church beside us, Tudor buildings on either side, and little shops with attractive bow windows.

'This is where I want to live,' I cried. 'We won't look anywhere else from now on.' And so began my love affair with Pinner, a love affair which has continued to this day.

Three weeks later we had found our house. Spring blossom of peach, cherry and almond was such a contrast to the asphalt background of Clapham that we felt we were in the land of Madame Butterfly. The owner was an elderly widow who was at loggerheads with all her neighbours, having reached the stage of eccentricity where she suspected people of getting up in the middle of the night and moving boundary stakes! So we were most warmly welcomed by everyone, who looked forward to having a more peaceful existence with two young busy people living among them.

A lovely little park was nearby, and the station was a good mile's walking distance. There was no bus service, but this didn't worry us, for we are both good walkers.

The house was semi-detached, Tudor style, with good-sized rooms, a nice garden, but badly in need of decoration.

I found it a bit dark, but agreed with the agent that lots of light paintwork would soon transform it. And for the first time in our lives we had a garage. No car, of course. But a lovely big garage which would be a great storage place for all our junk.

The only part I hated was telling Miss Chree. We were such firm friends that I felt I was deserting her. I knew she would miss our bedtime cups of tea, and our chats, and our sorties to the many London markets where we had picked up so many good bargains. In spite of her independence, she had grown used to having a kindred spirit within calling distance, and we were genuinely devoted to one another. She was like a firm, loving, disciplining adored aunt, and I was leaving her alone.

If she felt any of this, she said nothing, but threw herself with a will into helping me to assemble my accumulated possessions, ready for the 'flitting' from Clapham which I would see to, while Sandy held the fort at the other end, waiting for our Glasgow pantechnicon to arrive. With her vast experience of cataloguing antiques for 'the gentry', Miss Chree was a tower of strength. Curtains were packed and labelled. Ornaments wrapped in soft papers, packed, and the box clearly labelled. Typewriter once more secured in its travelling box. Bedding wrapped and labelled. Kitchen equipment, ditto. Right through everything I had acquired during my three years in my romantic roof-top flat. Was it only three years? It seemed like a lifetime.

Mrs Parker gave me the only laugh I had that morning. She came panting after me as I prepared to get in beside the driver of the van which was to take me and my treasures across London to Pinner. 'Have you got my horse?' she asked.

'Your horse?' I said, quite bewildered. I didn't know she had a horse, and I'd certainly never seen one. I looked to see if there was a horse standing outside, or maybe it was between the shafts of the van, like the old coal-carts we used for our Glasgow 'flittings'. It turned out she was referring to her clothes-horse, a rickety thing I hadn't used for years, having replaced it with a new one as soon as I had the cash to do so.

When she was assured her lame clothes-horse was safely stabled in the cupboard in the room upstairs, she let me go. She was well used to changing tenancies, but it was an emotional moment for me. She was my first London landlady, and I was grateful for the honest background she had provided for all those years. No great comfort anywhere, unless I saw to it myself, but honesty beyond price, and a concern for my wellbeing. All those masses she had said for me when my trains were late, that candle burnt to St Anthony when I'd had my handbag stolen, and that well-founded advice to speak to Tommy Handley next time I saw him, which had maybe led to the ITMA casting. I took her hand and thanked her for everything. I never saw her again.

When I reached Pinner, and the handful of stuff was unloaded from the van, Sandy was sitting on the bare floorboards and nothing had turned up from Scotland. I had to leave for the theatre, and he walked down to the telephone box with me, to make yet another call to the removal firm to see when he could expect our goods.

After the play that night it was the strangest feeling to be heading for Baker Street and Pinner, instead of the Underground at Leicester Square, and afterwards the mile-long walk to our new house through cool lanes of little houses was like a dream. I was exhausted, what with the morning's flitting, the journey to the theatre, the performance, and now the journey to this unfamiliar part of London, and I longed for bed. I wondered how much Sandy had managed to get done while I was entertaining the packed Friday-night house. I felt I was almost too tired to eat, and would just have a cup of tea, and leave all exploration of the contents of packing cases, and furniture till morning.

That was what I thought. When I got to the front door Sandy opened it, quite distracted. It appeared that the removal van had broken down somewhere between Carlisle and London and his last telephone call had resulted in his being told that the men refused to come out to Pinner that night and would not be appearing until Saturday! He was absolutely furious. He'd been sitting on bare floorboards all day, hardly daring to leave the house for a minute in case the van would arrive. So he told them we had nowhere to sleep and that if we went to an hotel they would have to foot the bill. With hindsight, we ought just to have done that and sent them in the bill and there would have been no argument. Instead, faced with this threat, they sent a rebellious crew out with the stuff at nine o'clock at night, and they simply unloaded the lot, and stuck it anywhere, without emptying a single packing case. Far from walking into a house with everything more or less where it ought to be, we couldn't even find the bed!

It was after 2 a.m. by the time we'd unearthed the head-board and siderails and spring from behind rolls of carpet and pieces of furniture, and when I fell into the assembled bed I thought I'd never move again.

On Saturday morning we discovered it was Whit Saturday and there would be a holiday on Monday, and we hadn't had the gas connected! I flew along to the gas offices and dragged a man back with me, protesting all the way that they ought to have been advised, and I went upstairs and lay down while he connected the gas cooker. There was only time for heating some pies and making a pot of tea before I had to get to the station for my matinée and evening performance. I didn't know how I was to do two shows, for I could scarcely open my eyes with bone-weary exhaustion. If it did nothing else, it made that long journey seem like five minutes.

I'll draw a veil over the following month or so, when the house was seldom free of painters, plumbers, carpenters and paperhangers, who consumed all my tea rations, and who held parties in our best front room, entertaining all their mates from all the other houses where they were working.

But at last it was finished, and to our eyes it looked simply lovely. It was the first time we'd had a room with casement doors which opened out on to a garden, and on hot summer Sundays it was sheer delight to stroll through after our meal and finish our coffee or our tea in the garden. Later, I found an excellent mason, and designed a wide crazy-paved terrace outside these casement doors and wide curved steps leading down to the lower garden, so that we could have all our meals out on the terrace in good weather. This was a great asset, and made such an impression on my mother when she came down that she thought she was living in a stately home! I had tried to describe in my letters how the dining room led via a sort of French window arrangement straight into the garden, but, having lived all her life in a Glasgow tenement of one sort or another, it was beyond her imagination. When she eventually saw it for herself she stood stock still in amazement and delight, for she adored gardens and especially trees. 'I juist couldnae picture whit ye meant,' she said. 'I couldnae picture it at a', but it's juist lovely. You can sit here wi' the doors open, an it's juist like sittin' in the garden, and yet ye're inside.'

She was enchanted too with her bedroom, overlooking the garden, and with the grand big bathroom, and, being used to the red and grey sandstone of Glasgow, was amazed at the English building their houses of 'juist ordinary bricks.' We had only ever seen bricks used for wash-houses or middens. We didn't realize our beautiful sandstone was something which was to be increasingly rare in building in a modern world. Like me, my mother fell instantly in love with Pinner, and declared it 'one of the nicest places in the world', and grew quite annoyed with her Glasgow neighbours for hinting it was a funny name for a place. 'I see nothing funny about it,' she declared loyally, although I had privately thought it a strange name myself when I first saw it.

But that first visit was a terrific adventure for her. She'd seldom been out of Scotland, and she thought it was like going to Australia, it took so long. In the following years she was amazed to discover the journey grew shorter and shorter, until she thought nothing of it, and when I went up and brought her back by sleeper latterly, she felt she had reached the heights of sophisticated travel. The idea of a man bringing her a little tray of tea and biscuits in bed in the morning quite affronted her at first, and her in her night-gown, and she was never quite persuaded that the man was far too busy to bother whether she had her teeth in or not!

Meanwhile Sandy had settled down to his job, and while the play lasted we only saw one another at breakfast-time and at bedtime, apart from Sundays, for I had left for the evening performance by the time he reached home from the office.

It was a very tiring time for me, for the play had now been running for almost two years; I hadn't had a proper holiday, apart from the abortive little spell at Leigh when I was still travelling to the theatre at night, and my convalescence in Glasgow, and I now had a house to run and a husband to look after, with all the shopping, washing and household tasks this entailed.

The others in the cast were dropping like ninepins too. Flu, bronchitis, tooth troubles, nervous exhaustion, we always seemed to have someone off, and at times we had all the understudies on stage at once, which made the regulars feel they were in quite a different play from the one we'd originally opened with. One night, as I rushed across to my adored school-teacher, she murmured, 'Fancy being in *Worm's Eye View* – all those years!' Fortunately I had no dialogue, so didn't feel like laughing, but it made me realize everybody was feeling fatigued with this interminable run. Margaret Rutherford had long since left us to do the film of the play, and Joyce Barbour had taken over for good now. The film company wouldn't cast any of us from the theatre, because they couldn't have afforded to lose the Wednesday shooting when we would have to do our matinée, and the theatre was playing to such good business the management wouldn't drop the Wednesday afternoon performance, so we all lost the chance of doing our original parts on film. It was a pity, and yet in a way I was glad because I felt we would all have dropped dead if we'd had to film the same play all day, and then come back and do it on stage again at night. Providence saw to it that we weren't tempted to this folly. I remember one night Viola Lyel saying to me, 'I'm so tired that I keep my eyes down on the way to the stage, so that I shan't see anyone and feel obliged to say "Good evening".' One of the actors burst into tears on his way to the dressing room one night, for no reason at all, and frightened the life out of me. I'd never seen a man burst into tears before. It appeared he was suffering from complete exhaustion and his doctor diagnosed such a low blood count that he would have to be given two weeks' leave of absence so that he could go and recuperate in the sun. So off he went to Portugal, and when he came back he said we all looked ghastly. He hadn't realized how ill we all looked until he'd come back to look at us with a fresh eye.

Maria had escaped from the boredom of the long run by going to America. She joined a house party there at the invitation of Tennessee Williams, and then went on to Italy for a holiday. What a glamorous life she was leading, instead of being cooped up with us in the small dressing room which had now been our background for the best part of two years.

When she visited us there she informed us we all looked 'old as God!' She looked like a million dollars, with her enviable suntan, flashing white teeth, and the latest in Italian fashion on her back, grey shimmering silk.

It did nothing for the morale of the rest of us to observe all this radiant health, which we looked unlikely to share in the foreseeable future. I tried to hint that every worker was entitled to a holiday break, but was pityingly informed, 'Not in the theatre, dear, not in the theatre.' It seemed terribly unfair, for now I knew that this was indeed most tiring work, and I'd reached the stage predicted by Eileen Herlie, where I was just conserving my strength all day and waiting for the curtain to go up. I found I could do less and less in the daytime, and marvelled at the strength I had had the previous year when I had actually had the stamina to go all the way to Wembley with Peter the schoolboy and watch the opening of the Olympic Games, and then fight my way on to a train with all those thousands of people returning to town, to do the evening performance. I felt I was looking back at my childhood self, and not just the Molly of a mere twelve months or so ago.

It was a very hot summer, and Sandy used to set up the garden hose when he came home and have showers in the garden, a ploy I could only join in on Sundays when I was at home. There were times when I treacherously longed for the lazy Sundays of Clapham when I could lie in bed half the morning, and drink endless cups of tea with Miss Chree, and not even bother to dress all day if I felt like it. Now, although every nerve-end cried for rest, I had to play my part in house-cleaning, gardening, walking, and all the chores neglected during the working week.

And then, suddenly, out of the blue it seemed, we heard whispers that the play was being taken off, because Tennents had another winner it wanted to bring in, and we were being sent on a long tour to capitalize on our success. When Duggie Stewart, who played Mr Sowter, told me that we wouldn't go on beyond September in London, my heart jumped for joy. I wouldn't have believed anyone if he had told me I'd be *glad* a play was finishing, but I hadn't had the experience of a long run then. 'Duggie,' I said, 'I'm not signed up for the tour. I'm not going.' When I'd been engaged, the agent prudently had not signed me for the following tour, if any, for he felt I might want to do other things than play a schoolgirl idenfinitely; and at that time Tennents had supposedly felt the part of Barbara wasn't all that important and could easily be taken over by someone else.

Duggie looked at me thoughtfully. 'Have you another job?' he asked.

'No, no,' I said, surprised at the question, 'I just want to be at home with Sandy. I can't have him come all the way from Scotland to be with me, and then dash off for three months all over the country and leave him in a strange environment.' Then a thought struck me. 'But do you think Tennents will ever forgive me?' Duggie had just lost his wife, and was susceptible to an argument which refused to accept separation lightly.

'Molly,' he said, 'you suit yourself. If you break your marriage, just for this play, and they don't want you for anything else in the future, they won't use you just to make it up to you. But if they *do* want you, they won't even remember that you didn't do the tour. In other words, they'll suit themselves too, so you do what is right for you.'

The management was stunned when I said in response to a lightly worded query, 'Of course you're going on the tour?' 'No thank you, I'm afraid I'm not.' I found myself sitting opposite the selfsame manager who hadn't let me home for the 'flitting'. After all his persuasive words about the value of the tour, of how irreplaceable Barbara was, as they'd found out when I'd been off ill, I found the courage to look him straight in the eye and say, in his own words, 'This time I'm afraid you will have to accept that my domestic responsibilities are your concern. My husband needs me more than the play does. I am not signed for the tour. I am breaking no contract. Thank you very much for asking me, but the answer is no.'

When the curtain came down on that last Saturday I had thought there might be some sort of final party, but there was nothing. Not even good-bye. We just removed our make-up, called good night to those still within earshot and went our ways. And some of them I never saw again. After two years of closest working partnership we vanished from one another's lives.

The bliss of being at home, with no professional responsibilities, was absolute. I didn't miss the theatre for one second. The phone was being installed and, believe it or not, the first call I had was to ask me to play Barbara out at Watford. I had felt I never wanted to say those lines again, but it was impressed upon me that the management here was excellent, had film connections, and other very good theatre connections and playing for them would do me a great deal of good. So I did it, and on the opening night I had a call from Pinewood asking me to do three days that week in a star-studded film and I had to turn it down! That's the way the luck goes in show business and, remembering Marjorie Fielding's advice about not thinking of jobs which escaped one, once a decision had been made, I tried not to regret this lost opportunity.[1] It was in this show that I met Sheila Scott, later to be the immensely successful world flier, following in the steps of Amy Johnson, but at that time she played my adored schoolteacher, and impressed me with her classic good looks and magnificent blonde hair. Her picture adorned all the Underground stations, advertising a well-known shampoo, her blonde hair flowing like a curtain in the breeze. In fact I couldn't believe it was the same person when I read of her aviation exploits, and thought I must be mistaken, but when I later met her at a Women of the Year lunch it was she who winked and whispered, 'It's a long time since Watford!'

We hadn't counted on getting any holidays, because Sandy had only started his London job in May, but the firm generously said he mustn't lose out on a vacation merely because he had changed his situation, and we found ourselves with a whole fortnight in October. Oh, how glad I was I hadn't gone on that tour, for we both really needed sea and sunshine more than we knew, after all the upheavals of the previous nine months. We chose Jersey, which was a much quieter island than it is now, and in October it was like my experience of the touring resorts out of season. Miles of quiet beaches, empty roads, splendid service in a partly closed hotel, and, best blessing of all, perfect weather. The sea was like warm milk at the end of this perfect summer, and health came rushing back as we bathed, and walked, and explored the whole of this beautiful island.

1. *A Toe on the Ladder*

There was an old lady in the hotel whose voice fascinated me. She was over eighty, with a high shrill timbre to her vocal chords, and she used to call over the balcony to the waiters, 'Is it time for my milk? I'd like it *very* hot tonight, with a biscuit.' Racing along the beaches, I'd imitate this high-pitched quality to make Sandy laugh, saying something like, 'Sandy, is it time for my bathe? I'd like the sea to be *very* hot this morning. With waves.' Sandy not only found this amusing (we were easily made laugh, indeed we were downright light-headed with being off the leash after such a long time without a rest), but he said to me thoughtfully one day, 'You know, you should remember that voice, it might be very useful to you some day for radio.' How right he was. But more of that later.

When we returned from Jersey, restored and refreshed in every way, ready to enjoy our new background south of the border, I decided to concentrate on radio for a while, so that Sandy and I would have more time together and he'd have the normal comfort of coming home to a cooked meal at the end of his day's work. I went to see my Children's Hour producer Josephine Plummer again and told her I was available. Indeed, I went the rounds of all the radio people telling them the 'glad' tidings, for under my contract with Tennents I hadn't been allowed to do anything on radio during the run of the play. This was in case people heard an actor on the air, and deduced he couldn't also be working in the theatre, and so box-office returns might be affected. Managements were unmoved by the argument that at the end of the cast lists in the *Radio Times* a note was inserted 'appearing at present in . . .' giving the name of the play. They refused to believe people consulted the *Radio Times* as thoroughly as all that, in spite of its having the largest circulation of any publication at that time in Britain. So the radio ban had remained. Till now.

Jo cast me at once in one of the Rudyard Kipling *Just-so* stories, 'How the Whale got his Throat', and I found myself working again with Fred Yule, who had been Bigga-Banga in ITMA. It was great fun, if slightly terrifying when I found that at the end of the play I had to read a poem *in English*, which was my way of describing having to deliver it with an English accent. Jo smilingly said, 'You can do it,' and seemed quite satisfied with my rendering.

Then the BBC decided that in memory of the great Tommy Handley that year's radio awards would take the form of 'Tommys', which would be presented during a lavish dinner-dance to be held in the Grosvenor Hotel in Park Lane, and to which all the ITMA cast, past and present, would be invited. The awards would be shown on television, and every celebrity in London would be there.

Even Sandy, who kept well out of the limelight, was stirred by the invitation to this great event. Park Lane was lined with crowds waiting to see the celebrities arrive, but I hadn't done enough TV or films to be a 'known face' and was able to slip in practically unnoticed, which was no disappointment, for I knew I was very small fry in this company. It was lovely to see Joan Harben again, and Deryck Guyler, and Hugh Morton; Diana Morrison and Fred Yule, and, of course, Lind Joyce and dear old Horace Percival. Before the awards we all lined up and were introduced singly to the audience, under the blazing TV lights and we each stepped forward to the mike and said our famous catch-phrases. It was very exciting to find ourselves applauded by that distinguished audience, and then came the awards, with our own Scottish Jimmy McKechnie, with whom I'd done my very first broadcast from Glasgow, taking the award as best radio actor of the year. A few of the top stars did a little variety act to complete the show for the TV audience, among them Bebe Daniels and Ben Lyon, who pretended Ben ought to have had the award for best actress instead of Gladys Young! And that was the first time I had seen the famous couple in the flesh, at close quarters. I *had* seen them once before at a variety show in the Palladium, but only as one of the audience.

Walking back to our seats after a waltz, we found ourselves right beside them. Sandy said to Ben, 'I saw you in your film *Hell's Angels*,' and Ben laughed and said, 'Well, they must have carried you in from your pram.' I can't even remember what I said to them, I was so overcome at finding myself there at all. And I certainly never dreamed I'd find myself talking to them much in the future. I truly thought this was a 'once only' when I was rubbing shoulders with the great just because of my ITMA connection.

Then it was back to Children's Hour, and a fine part from producer Jo Plummer, Rebecca, in *Rebecca of Sunnybrook Farm*. It's easy for the Scottish accent to cover itself completely in another dialect, and American was nae bother to me. I was always imitating American film stars, and I've also always been able to do a child's voice. I loved this series from start to finish, with its wide range of emotion, and the audiences loved it too, for it won the award as the best children's radio series of the year and was repeated by special request. I had dozens of letters, the most amusing being from a delightful old gentleman who wrote that although he and his wife were in their seventies, they were not yet stodgy, and had been so captivated by my roguish childishness and saddened by my harsh treatment at the hands of one of my aunts, they would love to offer me a holiday at their farm in Devon. I would enjoy glorious scenery, he said, unlimited milk and eggs for my growth, and a horse to ride if I so desired. If I found I liked the place, and took to them, they would be more than happy to adopt me and give me the love and care I obviously needed

Alas, I had to write back and reveal the awful truth that I had a husband, and wasn't quite so juvenile as the lively Rebecca.

Strangely enough, I had a reference to this lovely series only recently when I was up in Glasgow on a signing session for my recently published book, *A Toe on the Ladder*. A lady who had patiently queued told me that when she was carrying her first baby she had to rest a great deal, and had started listening to me as Rebecca. She had been enthralled both with the story and the quality of the character which came over, and made up her mind that if her child was a girl she would call her Rebecca, after the heroine of the series, in the hope that she would perhaps share the qualities of truth and courage I had portrayed. Well, it was a little girl, and she was duly christened Rebecca, and has grown up to be the joy her mother had hoped she would be when she listened to the adventures of Rebecca of Sunnybrook Farm all those years ago. I was most touched by this story.

Then came another schoolgirl part playing opposite Richard Hearne on TV. Although I was, in the words of Peter, my schoolboy opposite in *The Happiest Days*, 'an auld merrit wife', I was continually playing schoolgirls at this time. I was even tested for the part of the thirteen-year-old girl for the film *No Room at the Inn*, but lost this because I looked nearer seventeen! I was delighted to be told this, for I was considerably more than seventeen, and had thought I'd be slung out for daring to go along for the schoolgirl part, which I'd only done to please my agent.

Anyway, for this Richard Hearne playlet, I didn't know what I was letting myself in for. Richard, as you probably know, is a real acrobat and when he asked me if I minded being pulled about a bit, I said, cautiously, 'No, so long as it's nothing too violent, for I'm not an acrobat, although I'm pretty supple.'

'Oh, it won't be too violent,' he assured me, and during rehearsal it wasn't more than being pulled by the feet along the floor and dumped on my back a few times.

It was a live show, as they mostly were then, and when it came to transmission I was horrified to find myself caught by the feet, swung right off the ground, head downwards, and bounced up and down like a yo-yo, before being let go. My skirts fell over my eyes, revealing navy-blue bloomers, I didn't know *where* I was, much less where the camera was, and I staggered about like a female Charlie Chaplin on a rough sea. Everyone was in fits of laughter because my dazed stagger looked so funny, and the viewers all found it great fun, but I may say I carried several large black and blue marks on my torso for several weeks afterwards.

Then another film turned up, *Comin' thru' the Rye*, based on the life of Rabbie Burns, with Terence Alexander, later to play a leading role in the famous TV series *Forsyte Saga*, playing Rabbie. As it wasn't a musical comedy, I was aghast at the foreign director's idea that everybody in Poosie Nancy's pub should turn and kiss one another at a given moment. 'But nobody would do that in Scotland, at any time,' I protested. 'The odd kiss, yes, but not the entire pub – that's not true to life.' The extras were furious when he called out, 'All right, no keesing.'

'Spoilsport,' they hissed at me!

'It's all very well for you,' I retorted, 'you're English. Nobody will blame you for taking part in such a travesty, but they'd soon ask me what I was thinking about to let such a thing happen.' I took my duties as guardian of Scottish ways very seriously!

I was doing quite a lot of radio now, for every department. Children's Hour, revue, plays, schools, light entertainment, and had begun writing scripts for Woman's Hour. I had heard a talk about folk cookery and thought I could tell them about Grannie's Scottish economies and it was accepted right away. Little did I dream that one article would lead to years of script-writing for them, and be the basis of my first book *Shoes were for Sunday,* for it was the childhood tales which led to my being asked time and time again to get all the memories between hard covers. But that was in the future.

My mother was coming again to spend the summer holiday with us, and I'd just come in with all the Saturday shopping, before going with Sandy to meet her at the station, when the phone rang and it was producer Tom Ronald on the telephone. He was working on the recordings of Cicely Courtneidge's show *The House next Door,* and needed a Scottish voice next day to help out the regular cast. It was one of those pieces of luck which, unknown to me, was to be a turning point. And it was the merest fluke he needed me at all. It transpired that the lady who was in his regular cast was also in another show, which had had its date changed, and she was needed on the same Sunday as Tom was recording the Courtneidge show. When she had looked at the script and had seen the part called for a Scottish accent that Sunday, she suggested he replace her for that one day, as she couldn't do a Scottish voice anyway. This would allow her to fulfil her other contract, which was for a voice she *could* do, and Tom could probably find a real Scot.

Well, he did, and the Scot was me.

My mother was scandalized to find I had to go out to work on a Sunday, and her first Sunday in Pinner at that, and I made Tom laugh when I told him my Presbyterian mother thought Londoners a Godless lot breaking the sabbath like that, when they had all the rest of the week to work.

Some weeks later I met Tom Ronald in Bond Street. 'What are you doing just now, Molly?' he asked me.

'Nothing at all,' I said, 'I'm free as a bird.'

'How would you like to do a trial recording with Bebe and Ben?' he said. I gasped. 'You don't mean Bebe Daniels and Ben Lyon?' I said, hardly able to believe my ears. He nodded.

'When?' I said.

'Next Monday evening, at Piccadilly 1.'

'I'll be there,' I said.

I walked away in a daze.

First Cicely Courtneidge.

Now Bebe Daniels and Ben Lyon.

I broke into a run for sheer joy.

This was *marvellous*.

Every instinct told me that this chance meeting had been arranged by fate.

I couldn't wait to get home to tell Sandy.

I saw nothing of the other passengers on that journey home to Pinner, but the wheels of the train seemed to be chanting, 'You're on your way. To something very special. You're on your way. To something very special.'

The future was to prove how right I was.